© 2023
Author and Editor: M.Eng. Johannes Wild
A94689H39927F
Email: 3dtech@gmx.de

The complete imprint of the book can be found on the last pages!

This work is protected by copyright

The work, including its parts, is protected by copyright. Any use outside the narrow limits of copyright law without the consent of the author is prohibited. This applies in particular to electronic or other reproduction, translation, distribution and making publicly available. No part of the work may be reproduced, processed or distributed without written permission of the author! All rights reserved.

All information contained in this book has been compiled to the best of our knowledge and has been carefully checked. However, the publisher and the author do not guarantee the timeliness, accuracy, completeness and quality of the information provided. This book is for educational purposes only and does **not** constitute a recommendation for action. The use of this book and the implementation of the information contained therein is expressly at your own risk. In particular, no warranty or liability is given for damages of a material or immaterial nature on the part of the author and publisher for the use or non-use of information in this book. This book does not claim to be complete or error-free. Legal claims and claims for damages are excluded. The operators of the respective Internet sites referred to in this book are exclusively responsible for the content of their site. The publisher and the author have no influence on the design and contents of third party internet web sites. The publisher and author therefore distance themselves from all external content. At the time of use, no illegal content was present on the websites. The trademarks and common names cited in this book remain the sole property of the respective author or rights holder.

Thank you so much for choosing this book.

Table of contents

Legal information 1

Table of contents 2

Foreword 3

1 Introduction: course and scope of learning 4

2 What is Tinkercad? The first steps 5

3 CAD design with Tinkercad 15

   3.1 Basic information on CAD design 15

   3.2 Working environment: "3D Design" 17

   3.3 CAD project 1: Smartphone cover 45

   3.4 CAD project 2: Wrench 61

   3.5 Block-based Design with Tinkercad 68

4 Electronic circuits with Tinkercad 79

   4.1 Create an electronic circuit in Tinkercad 79

   4.2 Background knowledge – Fundamentals of electrical engineering 80

      4.2.1 Electricity 80
      4.2.2 Circuit 81
      4.2.3 The diode and the light-emitting diode (LED) 83
      4.2.4 The resistance 85

   4.3 Working environment: "Circuits" 86

   4.4 "Circuit" project 1: photoresistor controls motor speed 98

   4.5 "Circuit" project 2: Control RGB LED with an Arduino 100

5 Programming with Tinkercad 107

Closing words 121

Imprint of the author / publisher 125

Foreword

Thank you so much for choosing this book!

If you are looking for a practical guide for the very easy and versatile and also free program Tinkercad from Autodesk, then it was the right decision, and you are well advised with this book: "Tinkercad | Step by Step"! I am an engineer (M.Eng.) and would like to introduce you to the topics CAD design, electronics, and programming using the ingenious software Tinkercad simply explained. You will learn in this book the theoretical basics for the creation of 3D objects, for the design of electronic circuits and for programming. So, this book offers you a complete, easy to understand and intuitive introduction into the world of Tinkercad! No matter what age you are, if you are still in school, if you are already an adult, if you are a student or a retiree. The software is fantastic and can be used by any age group.

After an introduction to the respective working environment and how to use the functions and tools of the software, we will create 3D objects, design electronic circuits and learn block-based programming in this course. Using numerous practical example projects and countless colored illustrations, you will be guided step by step and in detail through the great possibilities of Tinkercad. This basic book is especially for those who have no previous experience with Autodesk's Tinkercad and would like to learn one of the topics without any previous knowledge: CAD design, electronics, or programming.

In this basic course, you'll learn everything you need to know as a beginner about the operation and functions of Tinkercad! Take a look inside the book and get your copy as ebook or paperback!

1 Introduction: course and scope of learning

What you can expect in this book and what you will learn

In this Tinkercad Beginner's Guide you will find an introduction to the topics: CAD design, electronics and programming in theory and practice. I am an engineer and will share with you my knowledge from my studies and professional practice, so that you will have an optimal learning success with theoretical basics on the one hand, but also with practical examples on the other hand. In the first chapters you will get background knowledge about the software Tinkercad, then we start with the creation of 3D objects (CAD design), then we design electronic circuits, and finally, we learn block-based programming. So, there is a lot going on here!

In this course, which is specifically designed for beginners, you will learn all the basics for the successful use of Tinkercad.

In a nutshell, this course will teach you the following in detail:

- The structure of the software Tinkercad and its functions and tools
- Operate the "3D Designs" and "Codeblocks" working environment to create 3D objects (CAD)
- Operate the "Circuits" work environment to use it to create electronic circuits
- To apply the block-based programming for the mini-PC Arduino
- Numerous sample projects such as smartphone case, wrench, Light controlled motor, temperature controlled LED, and much more.

2 What is Tinkercad? The first steps

Tinkercad is an online platform of the company Autodesk, on which you can realize projects of a technical nature. The term Tinkercad already contains the abbreviation CAD, which stands for "Computer-Aided Design". With the help of CAD software, you can create 3D models and objects. This software is primarily aimed at hobbyists, tinkerers, or makers who want to use the modern possibilities of a PC to make their projects – even in the analog world – a reality.

Tinkercad offers an intuitive and simple platform for creating 3D models. These 3D models can then also be printed out with a 3D printer, for example, in order to turn them into real objects. With Tinkercad, you can not only design or create objects, but the platform also offers the possibility that you deal with electronic circuits and the mini-PC Arduino. In a playful way, you can immerse yourself in the world of electronics and learn new skills easily. Besides the possibility to construct 3D objects and to design electronic circuits, you can also learn programming as a third possibility on Tinkercad. For this, you can use block-based programming on Tinkercad and get familiar with this field easily. What block-based programming is and how to use it and the other features of Tinkercad, we will look at together in this course step by step and in detail. So, Tinkercad can be used as an ideal platform for an easy and brief introduction to the topics: CAD design, electronic circuit design and programming. These are also the core topics of this course. We will look at these three topics in detail in the following chapters.

Since Tinkercad is an online software, you can't and don't have to download anything, you can simply work in your preferred browser. In addition, Tinkercad can be used free of charge. Based on its appearance, Tinkercad's target group is primarily children and young people. In my opinion, however, the program is also very suitable for adults, especially if you are a beginner. Just this simplicity offers many advantages and quick success in dealing with the creation of 3D objects or electronic circuits.

All projects are stored in the cloud and so you can access them from anywhere with a computer, cell phone or tablet via the Internet.

Tinkercad is, at least in the area of CAD design, only designed for relatively simple objects and applications. That's fine for this beginner course and for all beginners. If you are interested in the construction of more advanced models, I recommend that you also definitely deal with the CAD program "Fusion 360" from Autodesk, which is also free for private users, and the associated course "Fusion 360 | Step by Step" from me.

Create an account and get started

Before we can start designing, programming and creating circuits, we must first create an account on the www.tinkercad.com website. We do this by selecting the "Sign Up" button at the top right. If we already have an account with Autodesk, we can also use it to log in (then click on "Log In"). A page will then open where we can select whether we want to join a class as a student, or create our own personal account. In our case, we would like to create our own account. You can then register either with a Google account or Apple account, or also - quite classically - with an email address.

Tinkercad | Step by Step

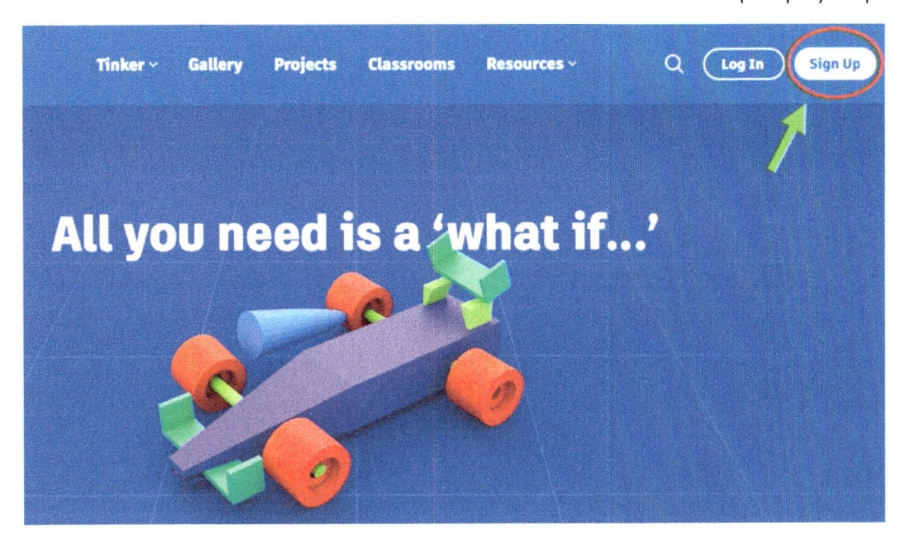

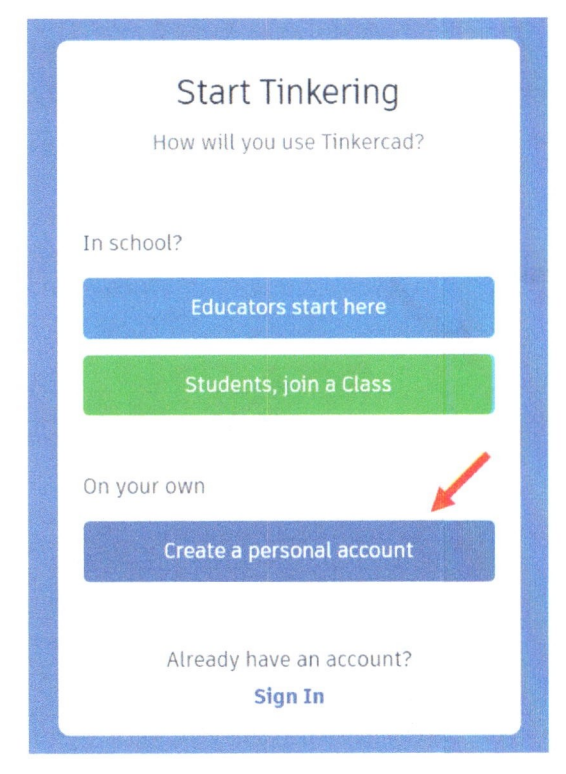

As soon as we have logged in, the start page of our account will appear in Tinkercad.

7

Tinkercad | Step by Step

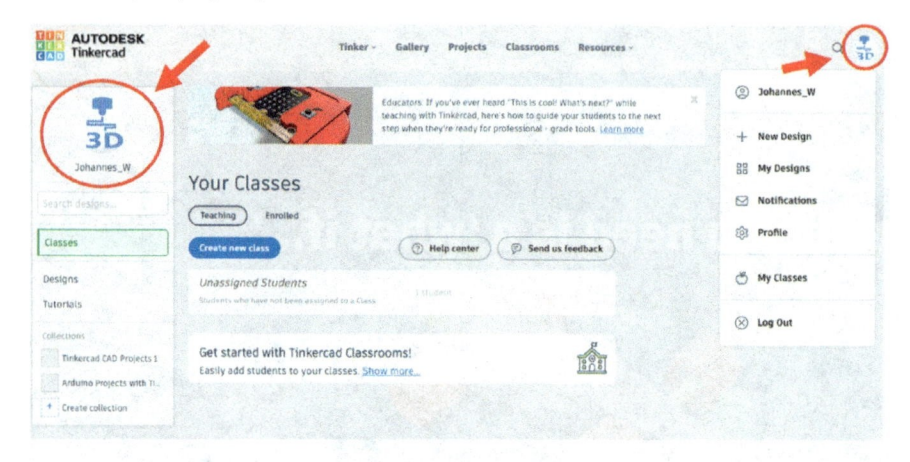

Let's take a brief look at how this start page is structured so that we can easily find our way around in the following. In the left area you will find the account name and an area for a photo, which we can upload individually. We can also find this again at the top right. If we click on the photo in the upper right, a quick selection menu opens. With a click on the photo in the left area, we can get to our account settings.

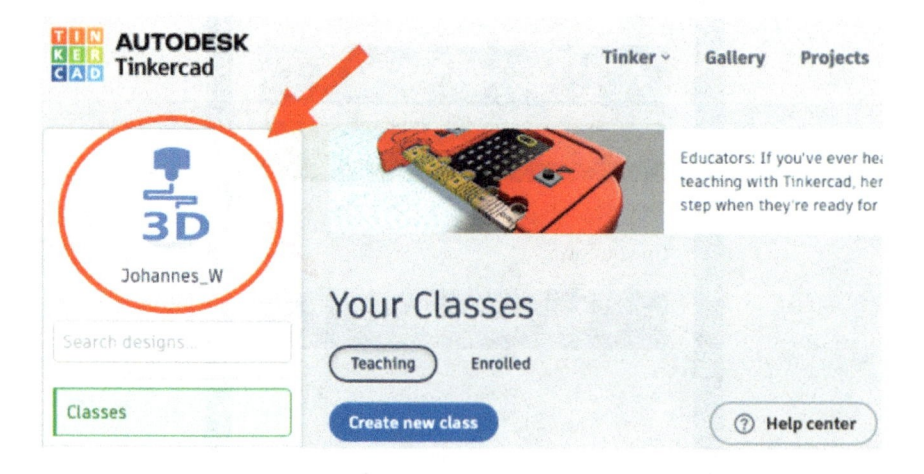

We get to a page where we can make personal settings. If "Personal Information" is selected in the upper left corner, we can upload a picture or logo on this page, as well as change our username, as well as make other settings. These settings can be seen by other users, depending on the privacy settings, as on other social networks. To save changes, we use the "Save Changes" button at the bottom right.

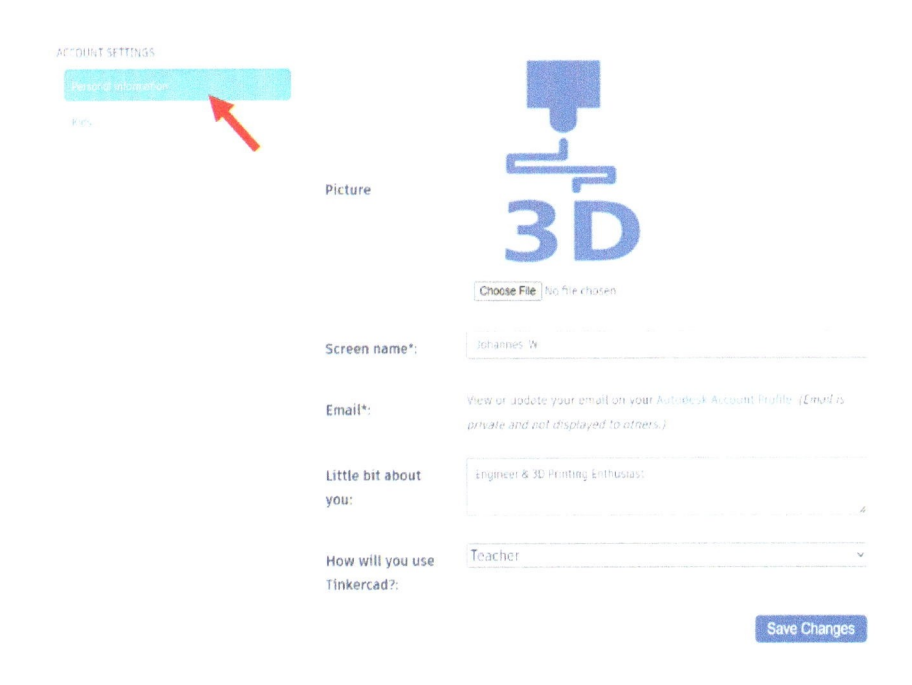

By clicking on the Tinkercad logo in the upper left corner, we return to the start page of our account. On the left side, below the account information, there are the sections "Classes", "Designs", "Tutorials" and "Collections".

If we click on the "Designs" button, all the files we have created will be listed. If you haven't created anything yet, nothing will be displayed here. By clicking on the button "+ New", which is located in the upper right corner, we can create a new file. Here we have the choice between "3D Design" (construction), "Circuit" (circuits) and "Codeblocks" (programming).

Tinkercad | Step by Step

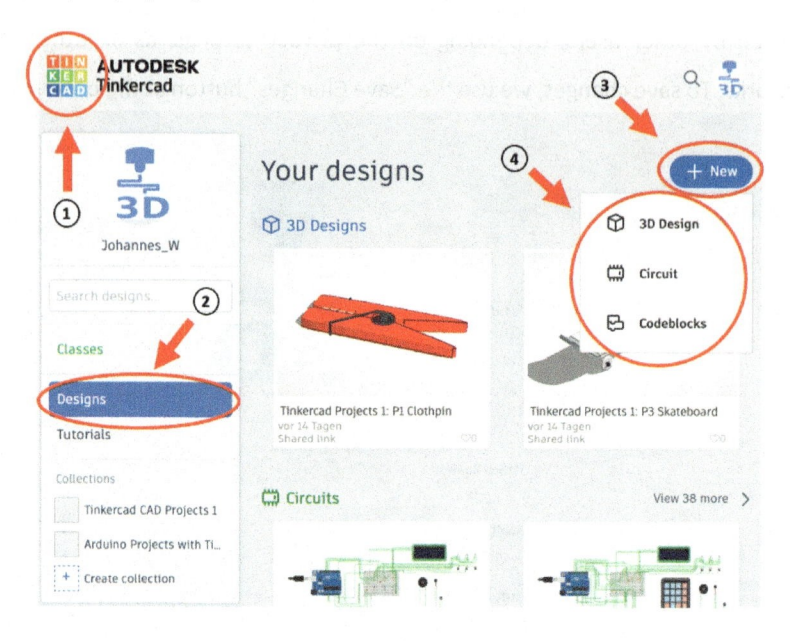

Let's take a look at an example design. Don't be confused by the funny name, I didn't choose it, but Tinkercad assigns these funny names (e.g. Exquisite Lahdi-Jofo) when creating a design. But we can also change the name. In the lower area of the created design we can see at which time we created the object, which visibility it has ("Private" = only the account user can see it; "Public" = all Tinkercad users can see it) and how many "Likes" or reactions from other users it has (small heart symbol at the bottom right).

Tinkercad | Step by Step

If you now move over the image of the design with the computer mouse, two options appear. One is the button "Tinker this" in the upper left corner, which means "work on it", and the other is a small cogwheel in the upper right corner. With the button "Tinker this", you open the design and can then edit it, we'll see that in a moment. Before we do that, however, we click on the gear wheel, which allows us to make the general settings for this design. When you click on it, a drop-down menu opens first with the options: "Properties", "Duplicate", "Add to Class Activity...", "Add to Collection...", "Delete". With "Duplicate" you can duplicate the design, with "Delete" you can delete it. We would now like to take a closer look at "Properties" and therefore select it.

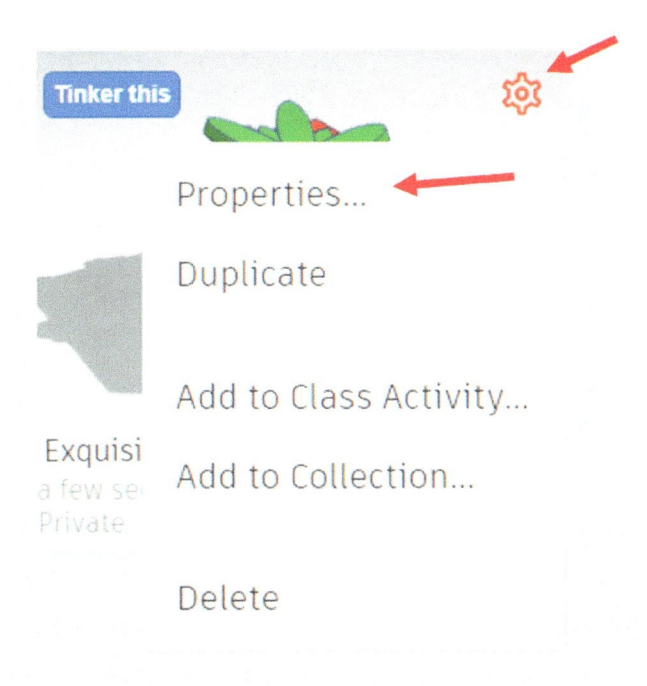

A pop-up window will open where we can change the name of the design and add, among other things, a description and keywords so that it can be found by us and other users.

11

Tinkercad | Step by Step

Design name

Exquisite Lahdi-Jofo

Design description

description to your design.

Tags (10 maximum)

Enter tag(s) here separated by commas. Press Enter to add a tag

Privacy

Please read our Be Nice Policy before sharing your design with our community.

Private

Not publicly listed, visible only to you

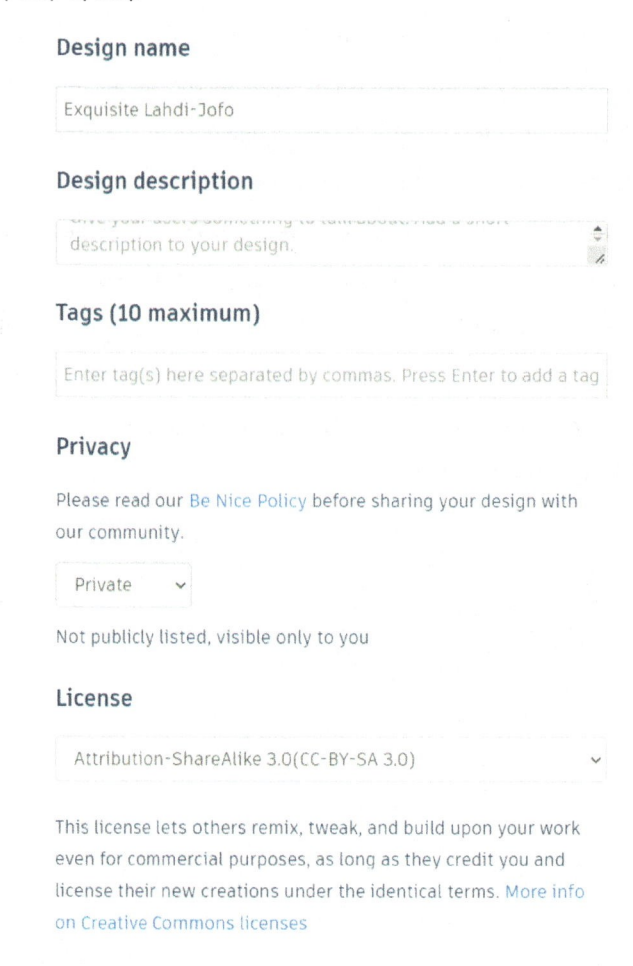

License

Attribution-ShareAlike 3.0(CC-BY-SA 3.0)

This license lets others remix, tweak, and build upon your work even for commercial purposes, as long as they credit you and license their new creations under the identical terms. More info on Creative Commons licenses

If we don't want our design to be publicly visible on the platform, we can set that in the "Privacy" section. In addition to "Private", i.e., <u>not</u> publicly visible, you can also set "Public", if you want to show your design to other users. Try it out if you dare, and wait and see what reactions you get to your designs in the form of likes or comments. In the lower area you will also find the section "License", in which you, as the creator of a design, can give a so-called "Creative Commons License" to other users and thus grant other people in an uncomplicated way certain rights of use, if you want. There are different licenses. Depending on the license, for example, only the use for private purposes is allowed, with another license the

Tinkercad | Step by Step

sharing and modification of the work is expressly desired and again with another even the commercial use of the work is allowed. In most cases, the author's name must also be mentioned in the case of public use of the respective object. Depending on the license, the name of the author must be referred to, or a link must be set in case of a permitted further distribution or representation of the work. The exact conditions of the licenses can be found at www.creativecommons.org. With the button "Save changes" in the lower area, we can save the changes and come back to the start page.

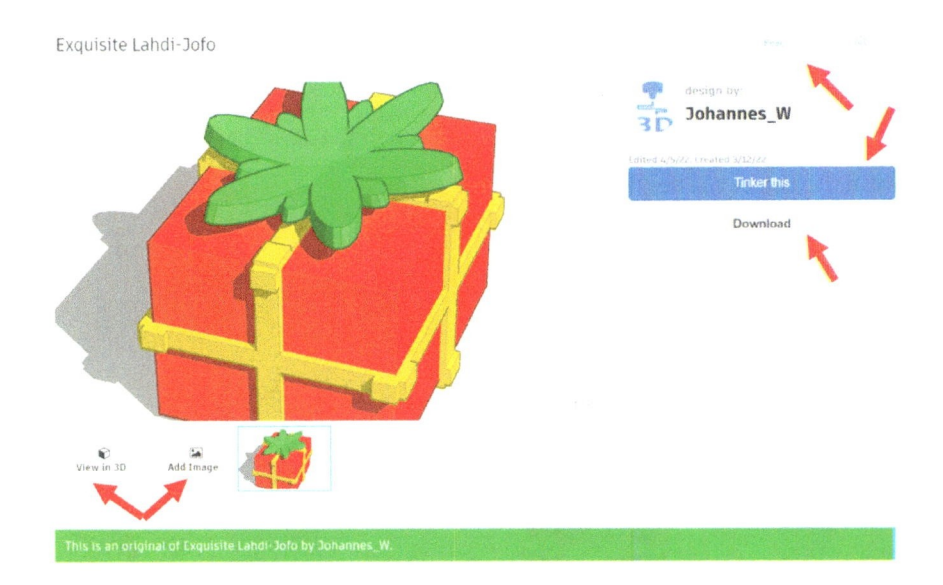

If we now click directly into the image of the design, an overview window opens, in which we have the possibility to edit it again with "Tinker this", or to download it, or to have it displayed in a 3D viewer with "View in 3D" in a kind of preview. We can also add another image of it here, for example, if we have printed the object. In addition, we can react to the design with various choices in the top-right corner and show our goodwill towards the designer. Of course, this only makes sense with designs from other Tinkercad users. If you want reactions, you have to set the design to "Public" in the settings and add a meaningful description and keywords so that it can be found.

13

Tinkercad | Step by Step

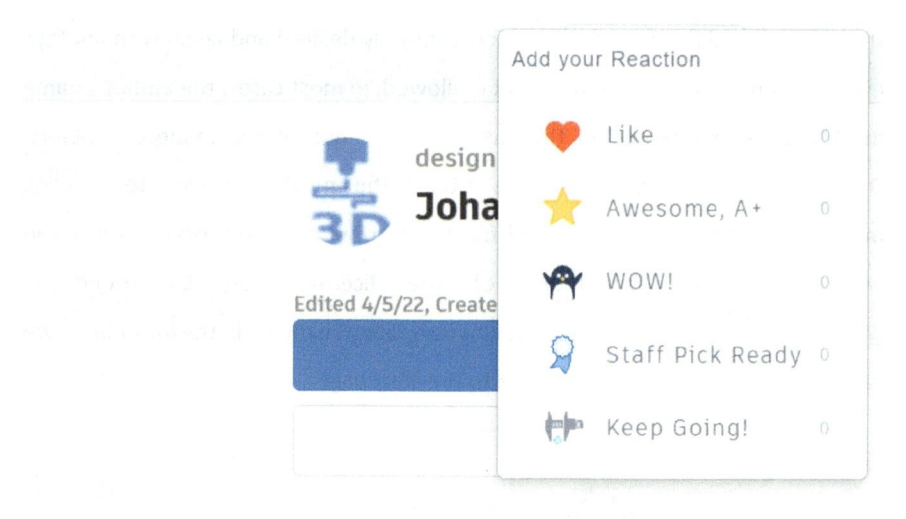

If we click on the "Tinker This" button, we can open the 3D design environment in which the object will be created and edited.

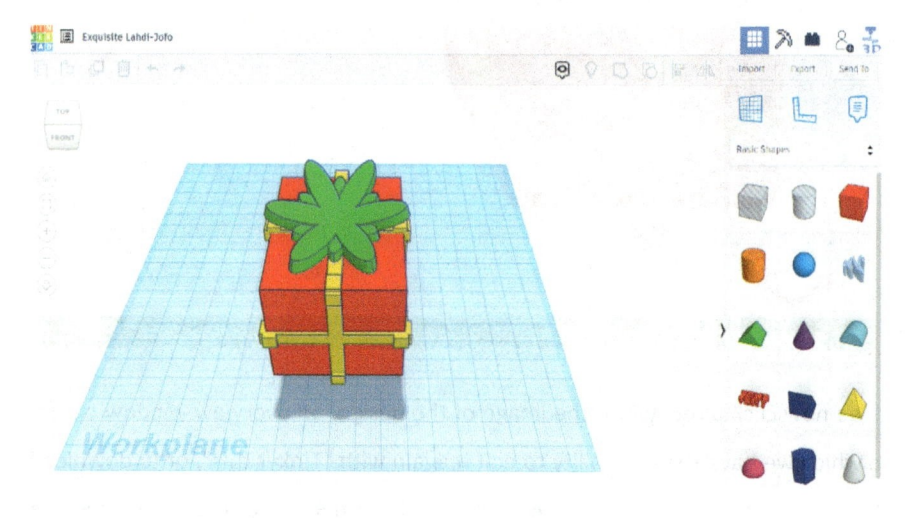

We'll take a look at how this works in the next chapter! Let's go!

3 CAD design with Tinkercad

3.1 Basic information on CAD design

Normally, a CAD object is started as a 2D sketch in a professional CAD software, such as SolidWorks, Inventor, or CATIA. From a sketch in two-dimensional space (x and y-axis form a plane), a 3D object is then created using various features and tools. For a cylinder, for example, you would draw the top surface, i.e., a two-dimensional circle, on a plane as a 2D sketch in these programs and then transform it into a cylinder in 3D mode.

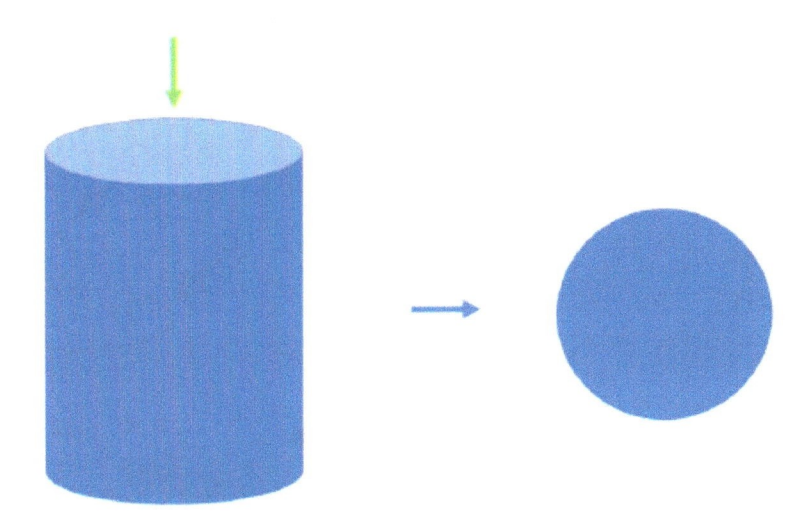

This type of CAD design is used (not only) by professional users, such as engineers or technicians, in their everyday work. However, since the previously mentioned programs usually cost several thousand euros per year, this is not an option for occasional private users. A good and free alternative is, for example, the license for private users for the program Fusion 360 from Autodesk. Here, the range of functions is very extensive and almost comparable to professional CAD licenses. However, the use of Fusion 360 is much more complex and involves several steps. If you have never heard of CAD design, and only want to design simple objects

Tinkercad | Step by Step

occasionally, the entry into a complex program is often not worth it. In this case, one should first deal with Tinkercad. Tinkercad is ideal for the entry into the world of 3D object creation and offers through the extremely simple handling, fast learning success and a very easy construction of objects.

In contrast to professional CAD programs, in Tinkercad you do not create a 3D object from a 2D sketch using 3D tools, but from simple, already existing 3D basic bodies, the so-called "basic shapes". We will look at the procedure for doing this in detail in this lesson. In order to do that, we first want to create a new design. We can do this easily on the start page by clicking the "+ New" button and selecting the "3D Design" option. To do this, we need to be in the "Designs" tab on the left.

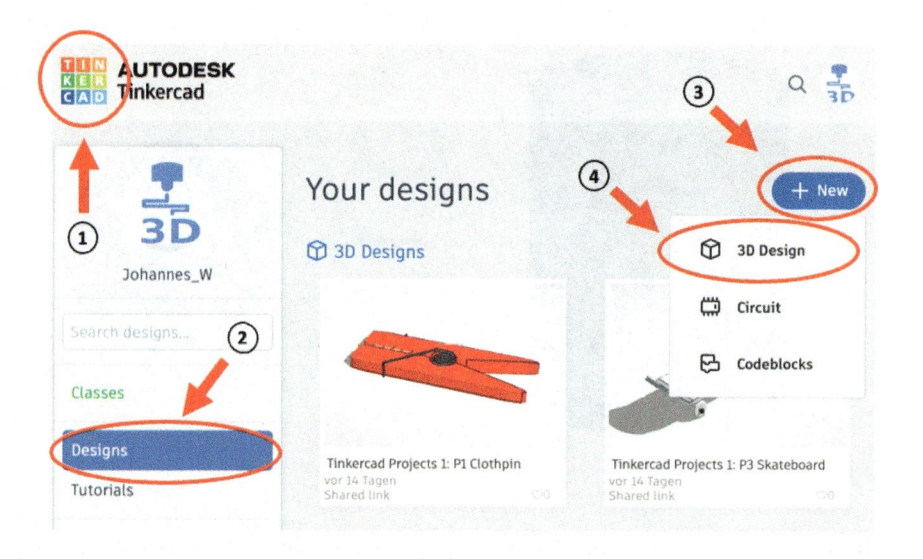

16

3.2 Working environment: "3D Design"

Once we have created a new 3D design, the workspace for creating and modifying 3D objects opens.

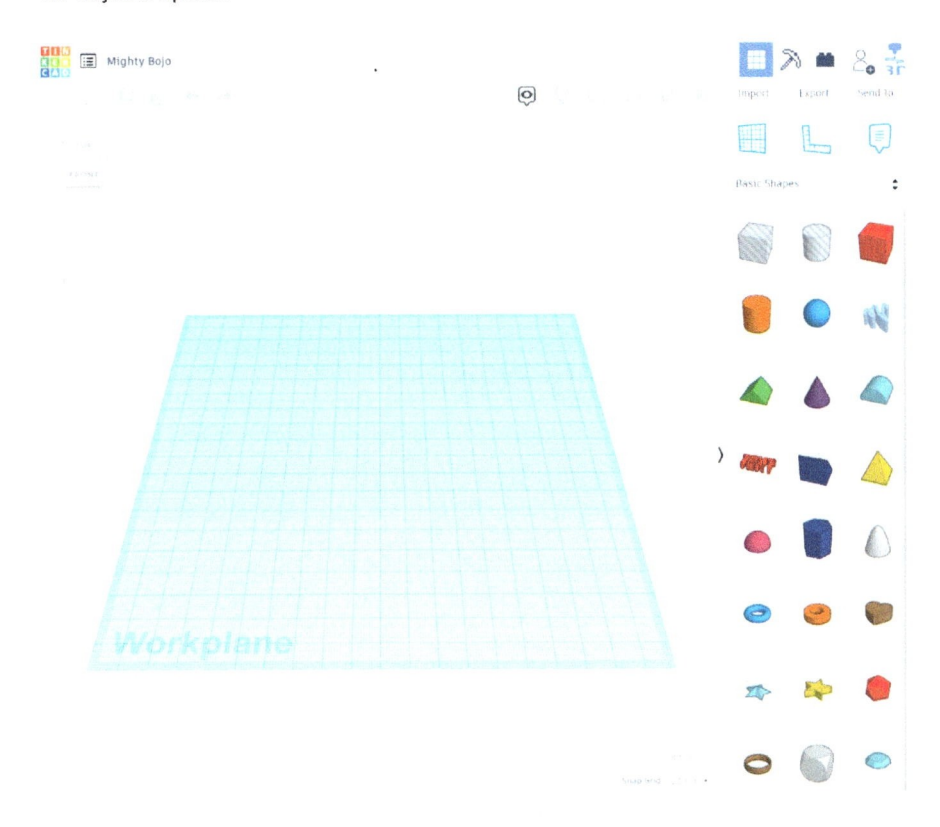

Before we create our first object and then move on to various CAD projects that we will design together step by step, we will first take a look at the working environment and its functions.

The light blue grid area labeled "Workplane" is our work plane where we build our 3D models. Think of it simply as a worktable where you place models and model them. With the help of the computer mouse, you can rotate and zoom this plane. For zooming, we use the mouse wheel as usual. To rotate the layer in any direction and view, we should hold down the right mouse button and at the same time make a movement with the mouse. And if we hold down the mouse wheel and move the

Tinkercad | Step by Step

mouse at the same time, we can move the layer. If we keep the left mouse button pressed and move the mouse, a red frame appears, with which we can select an object.

In the area on the left, upper side there is a small cube, with which you can also turn the view as it suits you. To do this, simply click on the cube with the mouse, hold down the mouse button and rotate the cube. Alternatively, you can click on one of the faces of the cube, e.g., "Top" or "Front", if you want to view your object from above, or from the front, or even from another side.

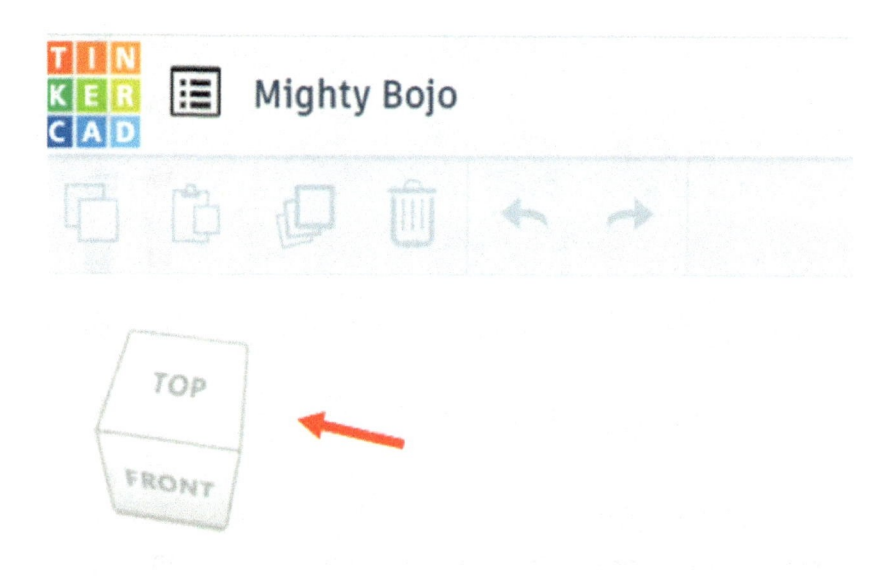

Below the cube, there is a bar that can also be used to control the orientation of the view. With a click on the small house icon, you can switch to a defined view, the "Home view".

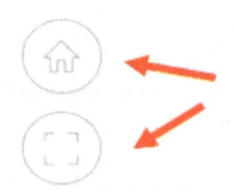

Tinkercad | Step by Step

With the rectangle icon below, you can fit all objects into one view ("Fit all in View"). But this is only interesting when you have created larger objects. The symbols for + and - are used for zooming. And with the symbol below, you can switch the view between "orthographic" and "perspective". What this means exactly, you can see best by trial and error.

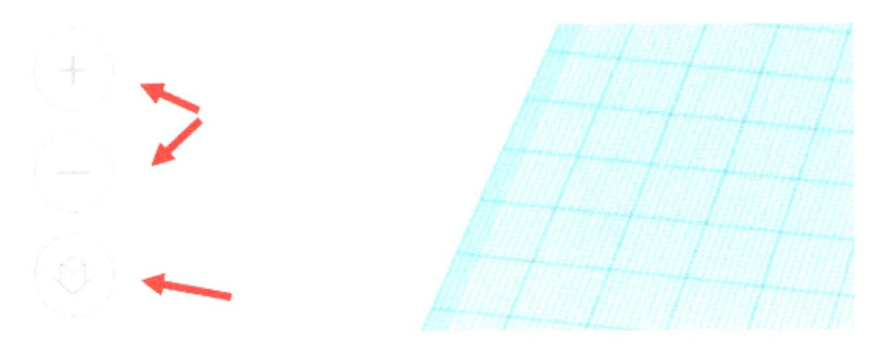

Now it's time to create our first 3D object. At first, this 3D object will simply be a cube so that we can still get to know the further setting options and functionalities of the working environment. Later we will create a few more complex objects.

To create an object, we can work with the already existing objects. Simple objects, we can find in the "Basic Shapes" drop-down menu. To place an object on the work plane, we simply click on an object, e.g., the red cube, and then move on the light blue plane. With one click, we can place or create the cube at the right position for us. By the way, if the selection menu on the right side is not displayed, it is hidden. With a click on the small arrow in the middle on the right, you can show it again.

If you click on the small star in the upper-right corner, the shape will be assigned to your favorites. You can find your favorite shapes faster this way.

19

Tinkercad | Step by Step

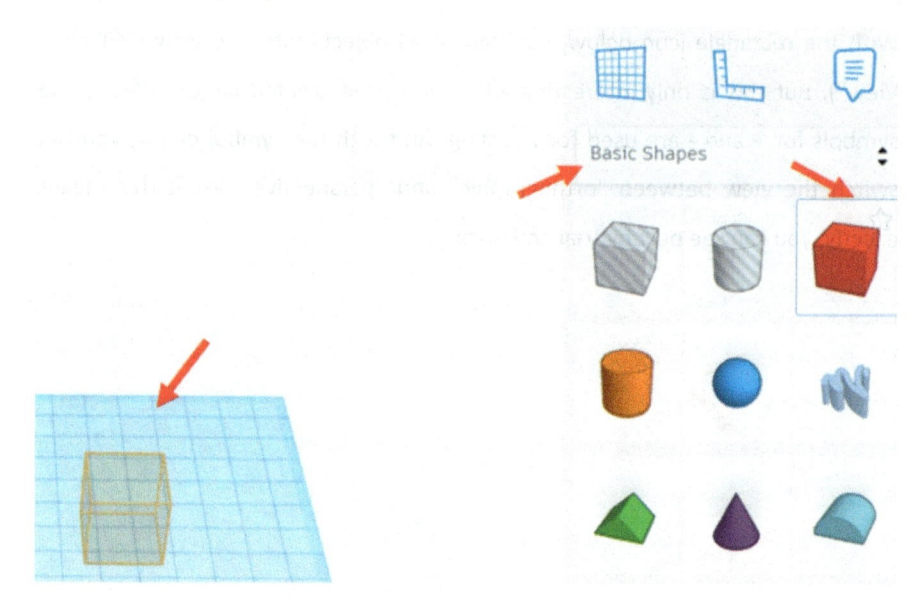

Once we have placed the cube or other shape, the settings for the object will open.

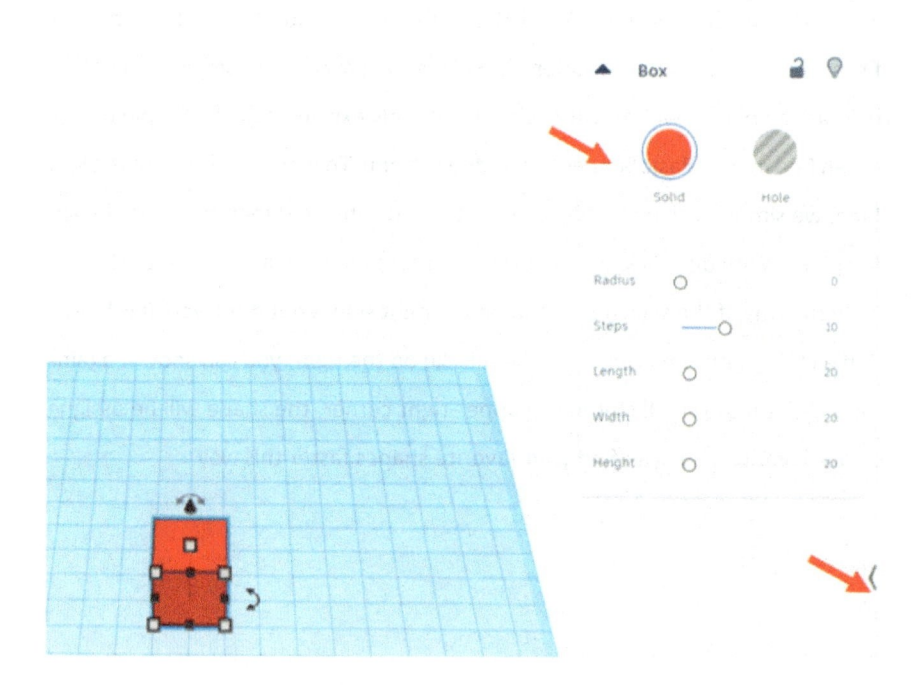

In the settings, you can define whether it should be an adding object ("solid") or a subtracting object ("hole"). The difference is that with "solid" you can add material
20

in the form of the object to another object, and with "hole" you can take material in the form of the object away from another object. What this means exactly and how you can imagine it, we will see later in detail with an example. But first, let's continue with the other setting options. For example, you can also determine whether the object or its edges should have a radius (rounded edges) and how long, how wide and how high the object should be. Just try all the controls once and see what happens. In the upper-right area, you can use the lock icon to protect the object from further editing by locking it with a click on it, or unlock it again for editing by unlocking it. With the light bulb icon, you can make the object disappear.

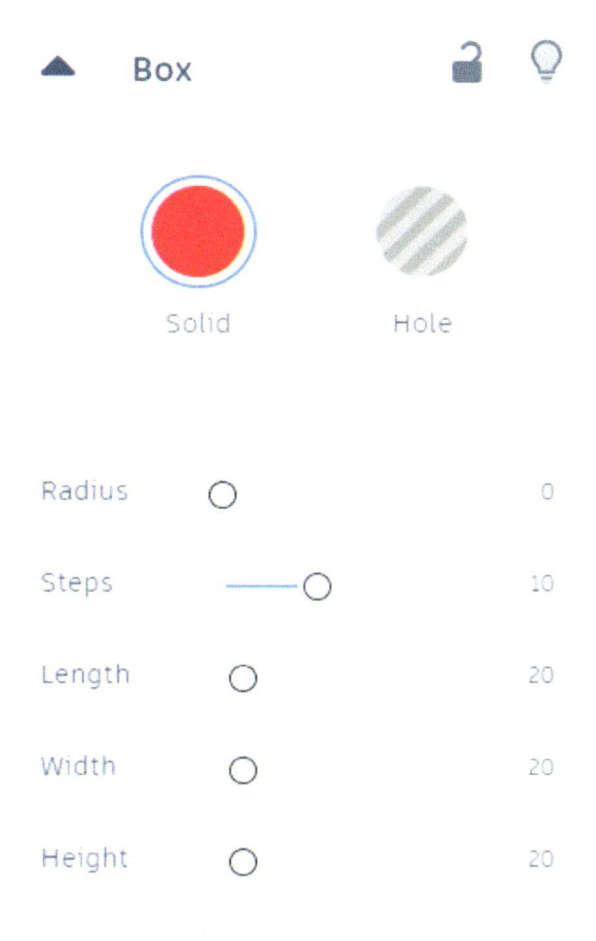

Box

Solid   Hole

Radius	○	0
Steps	──○	10
Length	○	20
Width	○	20
Height	○	20

Tinkercad | Step by Step

Before we move on to other shapes, let's take a look at three tools located above the shapes.

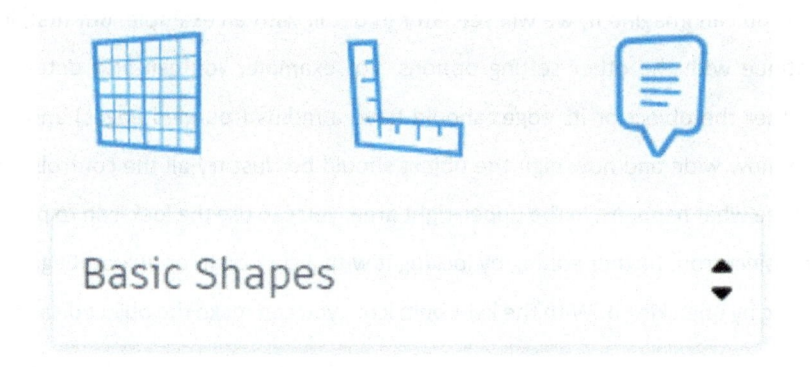

These are the "Workplane tool" (left), the "Ruler tool" (center) and the "Notes tool" (right). With the "Workplane tool" you can create a second work plane. Just click on it and place it, e.g., on the top of our cube.

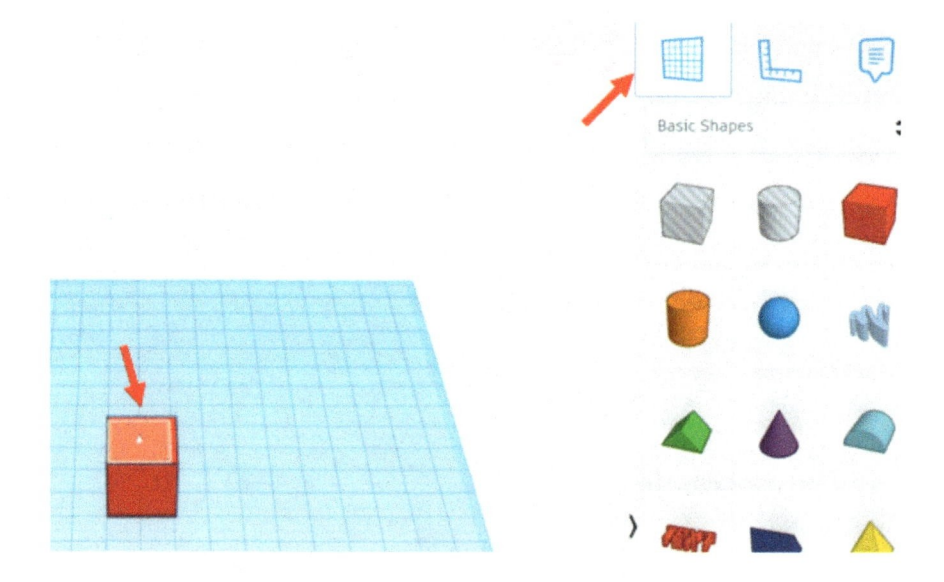

22

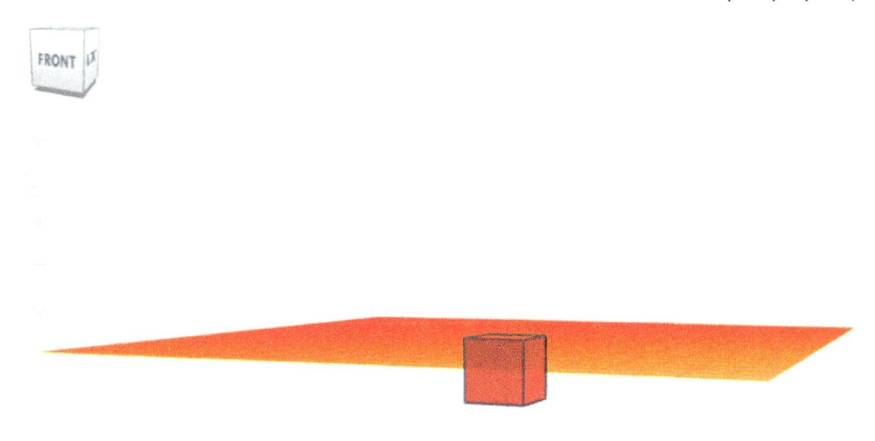

This creates a second working plane. The second plane is parallel to the clicked surface (cube surface) and offset from the first plane by a distance. For example, here we have clicked the surface of the cube, which means that the distance is one cube height. Think and try also once, what happens, if you click the side surface of the cube!

On this second working plane, you could then place another cube, for example.

With the "Ruler tool" you can place a ruler. Simply click, move to the work plane and select an origin for placing the tool.

Tinkercad | Step by Step

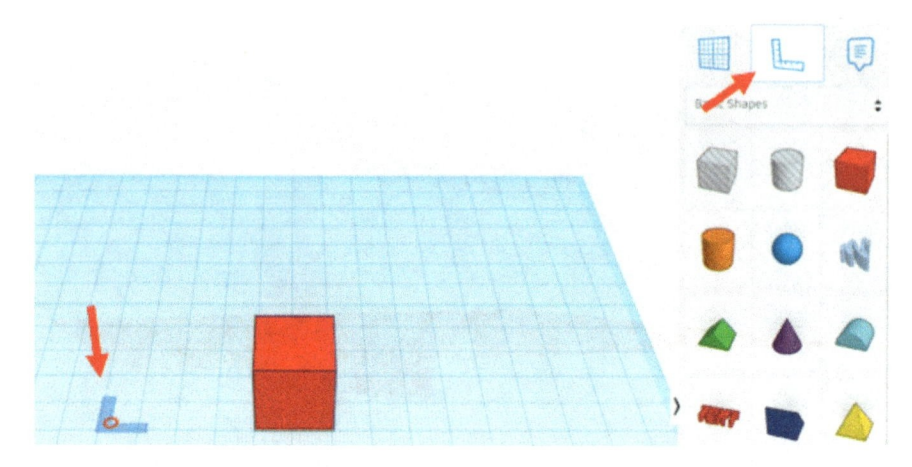

A coordinate system will then appear, allowing you to see the dimensions when you select an object (by clicking on it).

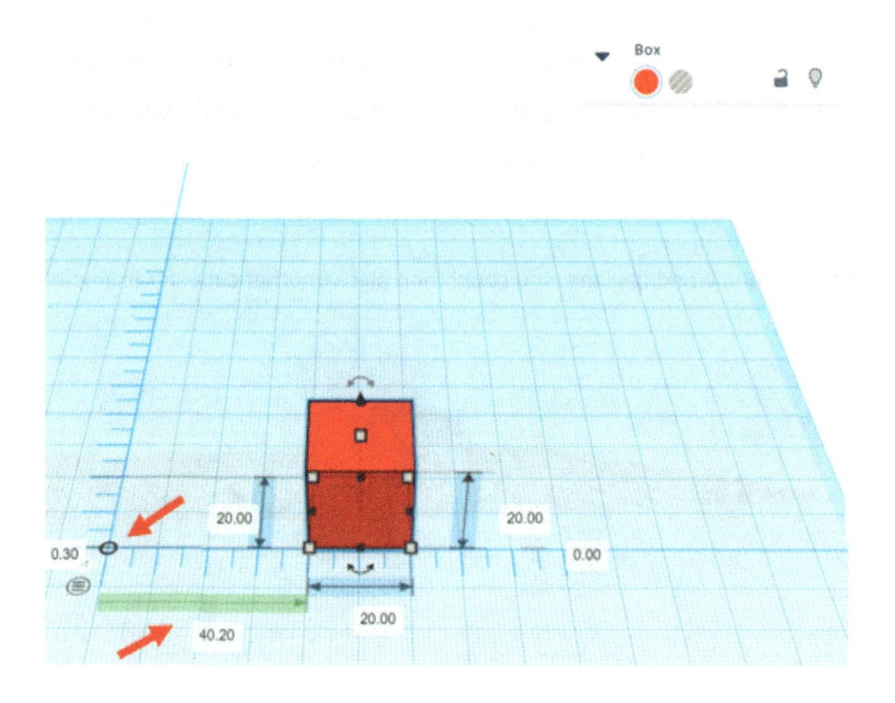

The distance to the origin of the coordinate system or the "Ruler tool" is 40.2 mm here, for example. In addition, the edge length of the cube can be read with 20 mm. By clicking on the origin (circle) of the "Ruler tool" you can mirror it (just try it). The dimensions here are always in "mm" (conversion to cm: value in mm * 0.1 = value in cm).

Finally, you can create a note with the "Notes tool", but this is very self-explanatory (just click on the work plane and enter text).

By the way, if you click on "Edit Grid" in the lower-right area, you can make settings for the workplane. You can change the units here, but it is recommended to leave them with "Milimeters". You can also set the size of the workplane. At the moment it is 200 mm wide and 200 mm long. Under "Presets" you can adopt the presets of certain devices, such as 3D printers. This makes sense if you want to print the object later.

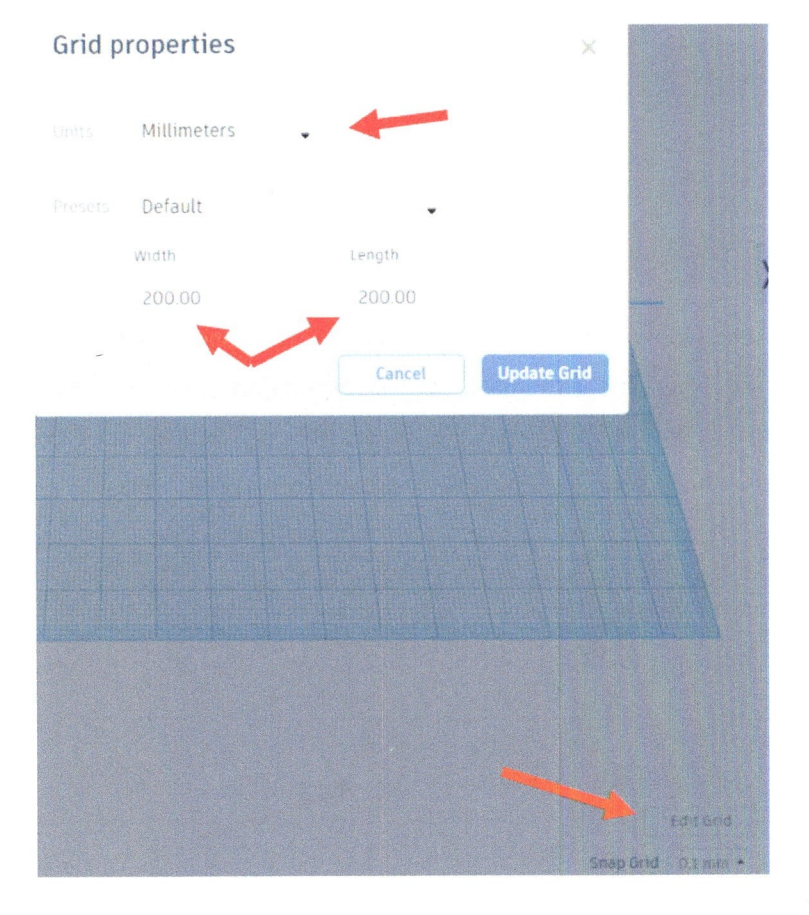

Tinkercad | Step by Step

In the selection menu of "Snap Grid" (below "Edit Grid" ; bottom right) you can set the steps in which the objects should move in relation to the grid of the working plane during a move. The lower this value is set, the finer you can move an object. In our case, for example, in 0.1 mm intervals, i.e., exactly around one of the small boxes of the grid. If we want to move completely detached, we can also set "Off" here and are then not bound to the boxes of the grid.

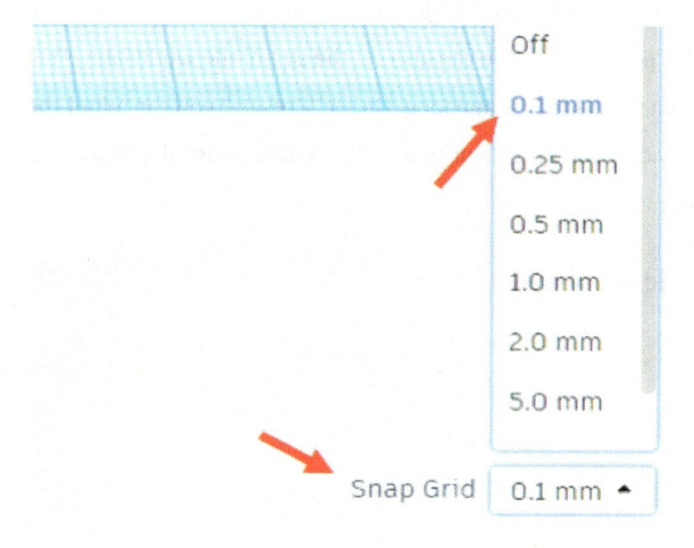

Besides the simple shapes like cube, cylinder, sphere, cone, pyramid and so on, there are other and also more complex objects that we can tinker with immediately. We can find them in the "Shapes Library", which we open simply by clicking on the drop-down menu we are currently in, e.g., "Basic Shapes".

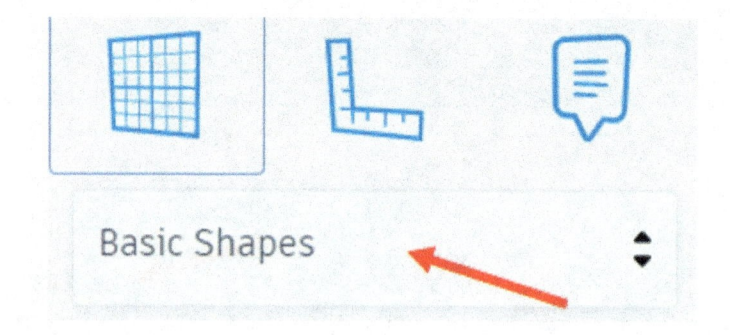

26

Tinkercad | Step by Step

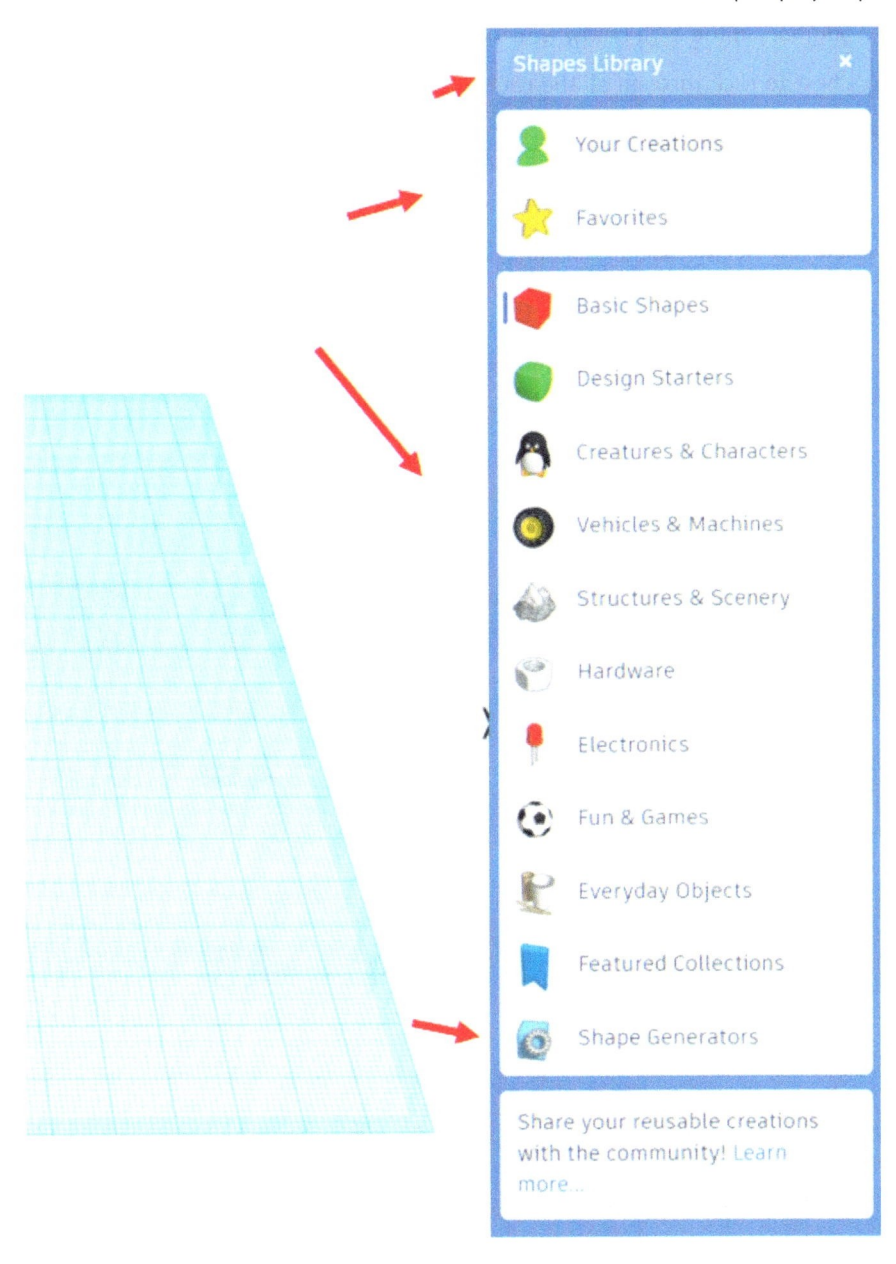

Here, in the upper area, we find the menu for our own saved creations as well as the menu for the objects marked as favorites.

27

Tinkercad | Step by Step

In addition, in the area below, you will find a variety of other categorized objects. It's best to click through all the categories once and see the objects for them to know what all is available.

A special feature in this area is the lowest category "Shape Generators", which we would now like to take a closer look at.

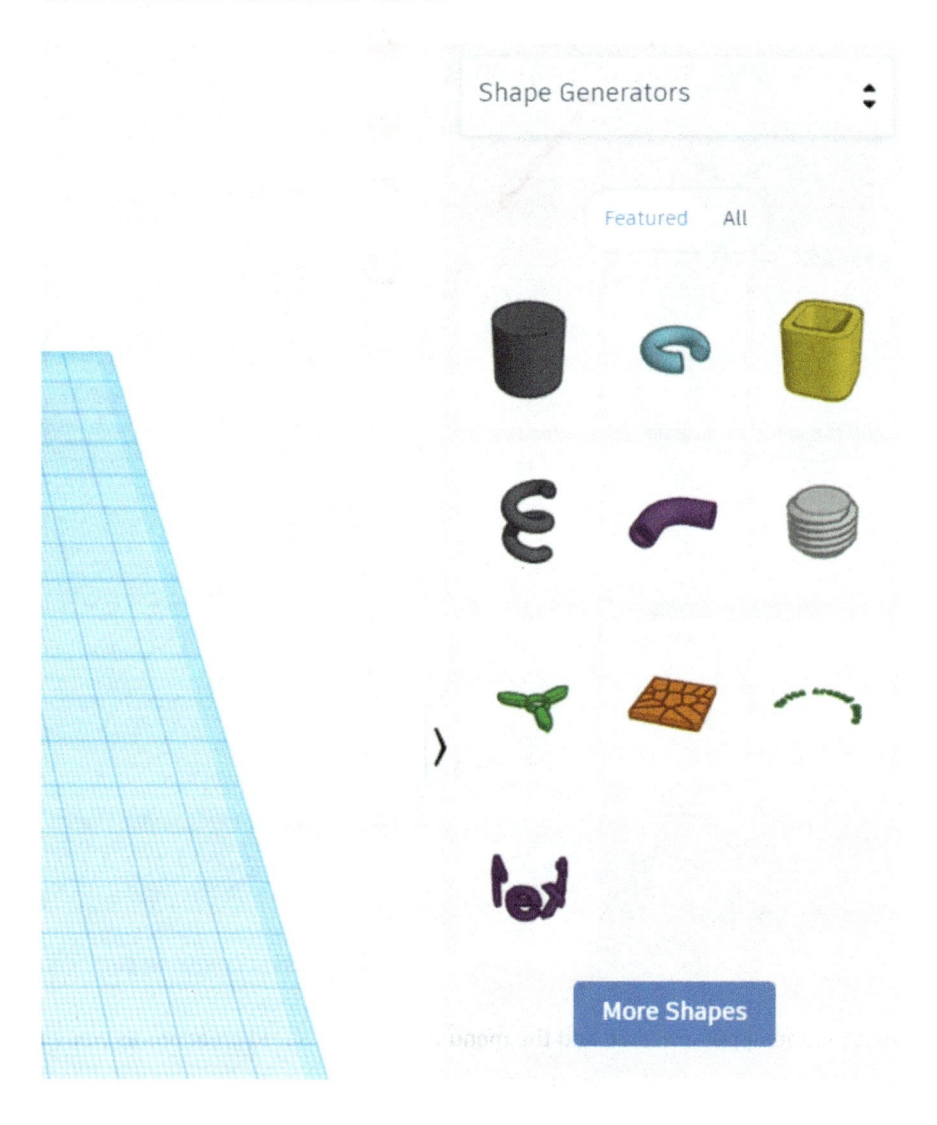

Tinkercad | Step by Step

In this category, you can create your own shapes based on existing objects by modifying them. For example, with the "Featured" selection you can find a bent pipe, for which you can make various changes in shape, diameter, wall thickness, and so on, using the settings.

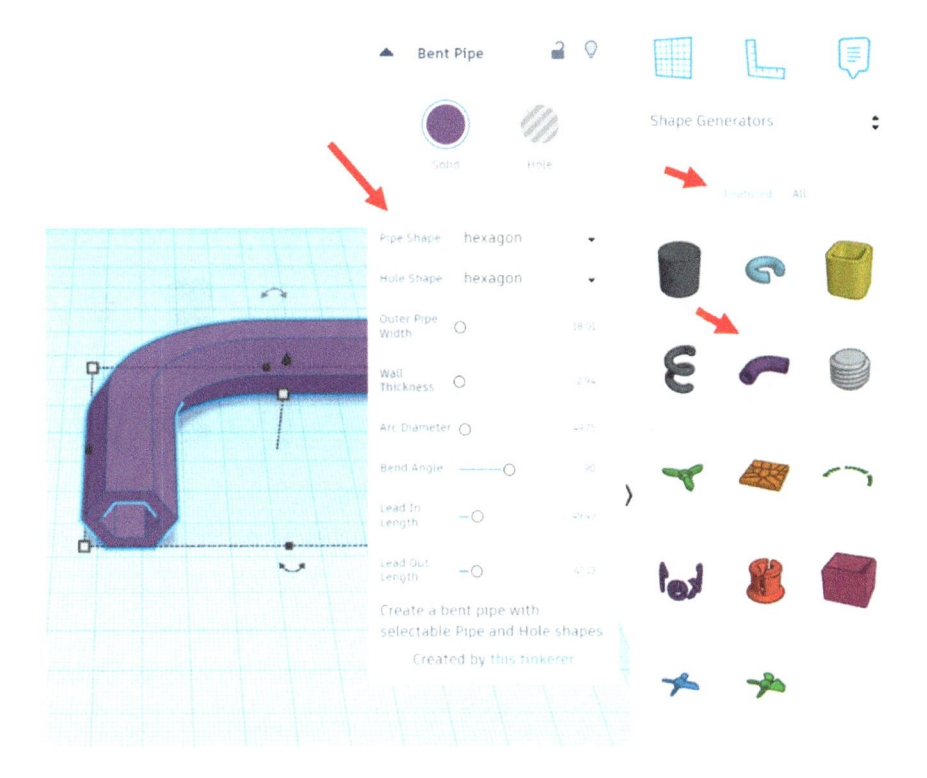

Many other shapes that can be modified can be found by clicking on "All". If you scroll down a bit, you will find, for example, a gear wheel that you can change as you wish. At this point, it's best to try out the possibilities of changing a few shapes. You'll see that there are different settings for each object, tailored to that particular object.

29

Tinkercad | Step by Step

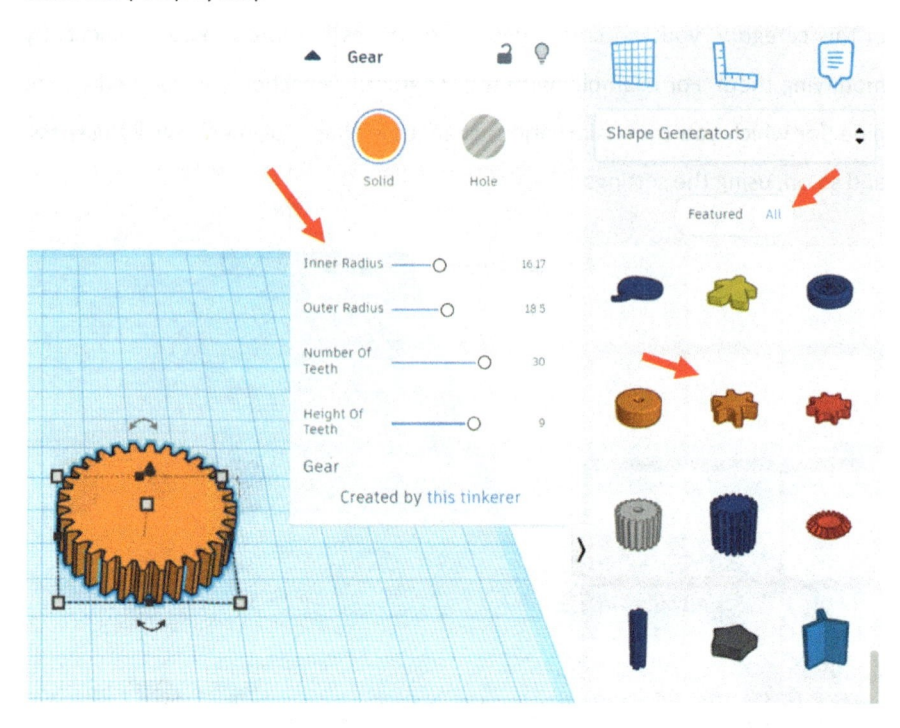

To save our new object as our creation, we then switch to the "Your Creations" menu.

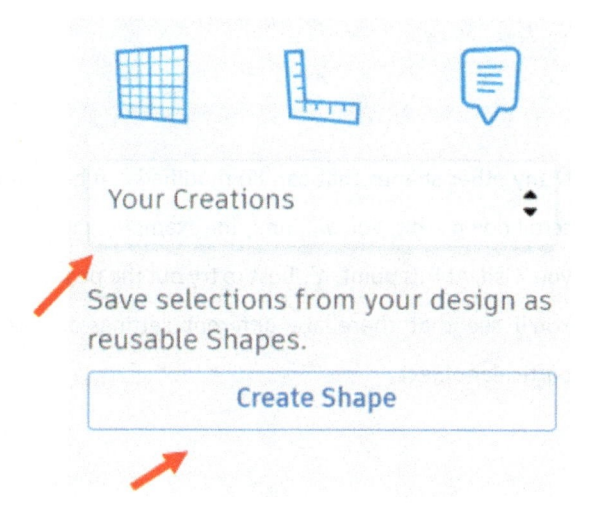

Tinkercad | Step by Step

Here, we can save created objects as particular shapes to reuse later. To do this, we first select the object to be saved, e.g. the modified gear wheel, and then click on the "Create Shape" button.

Then a preview window opens for the object, in which we can assign a name and a description, as well as keywords for easier finding. We can also set whether the object should be treated as a positive element, i.e., as a full body ("solid"), or a negative element ("hole") and whether scaling should be allowed or not. We will also take a look at what the "solid" or "hole" setting is all about. With "Save Shape" we can save our creation.

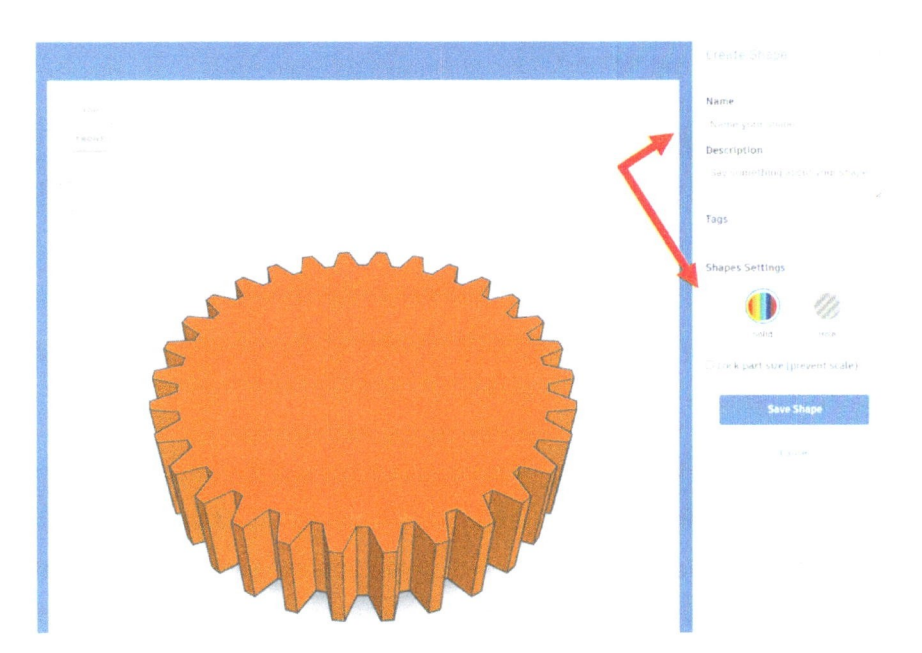

Lastly, we'll deal with the two bars in the upper area and then move on to the construction of objects. Stay tuned, soon we will create the first great objects.

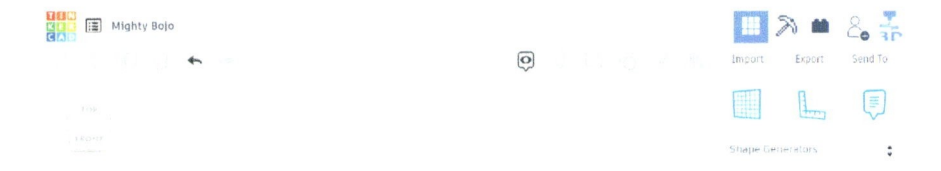

31

Tinkercad | Step by Step

On the left side of the upper bar there are general functions, which are also known from the classic programs. These are: Copy, Paste, Duplicate, Delete and Undo/Redo. To be able to select them, you must first select an object. You can select multiple objects by expanding a rectangular selection window with the left mouse button pressed.

On the right side there are functions that you need to work with 3D objects.

Import   Export   Send To

You can find here from left to right: "Toggle notes visibility", "Show all", "Group", "Ungroup", "Align" and "Mirror".

With the first two, you control the view of comments (show or not show) and the objects (if you have hidden one or more objects in the settings with a click on the light bulb symbol, you can show all objects again here). Now we will take a closer look at "Group" and "Ungroup".

With these two functions, you can connect and disconnect objects. These are two essential functions for the construction in Tinkercad.

Let's take a look at the following example with two cubes and two cylinders. For one of the two cylinders "solid" was selected in the settings, for the other one "hole". The dimensions do not matter and can be chosen freely, only the height of the cylinders should be slightly higher than the height of the cubes.

In the following, we will learn the difference between the possible properties "solid" and "hole" with the help of the "Group" function.

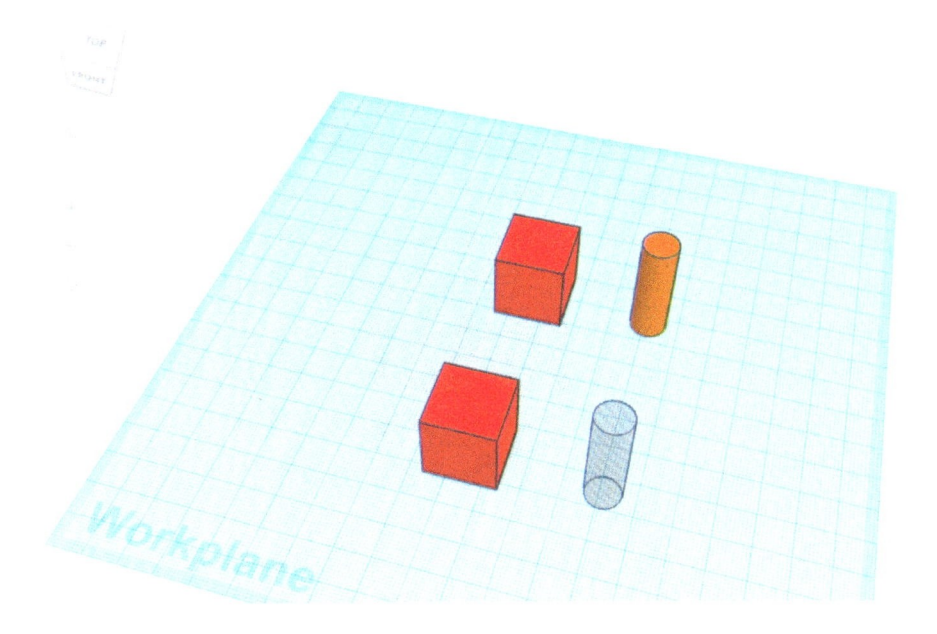

The two functions "Group" and "Ungroup" are very easy to understand. With one function, you can join two or more objects together, with the other one you can separate them. Imagine, for example, as if you were merging two objects. In the following we want to connect the objects with each other. To do this, we first drag the two cylinders to the left into the center of the cubes.

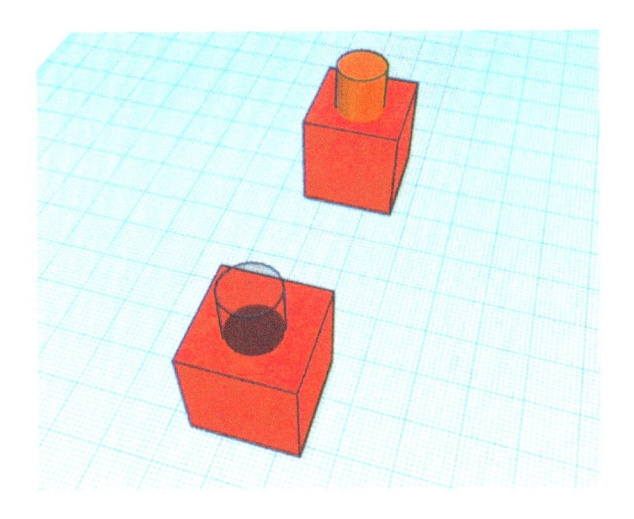

Tinkercad | Step by Step

Then we first select the two front objects (cube and cylinder with the setting "hole") and mark them with the left mouse button pressed.

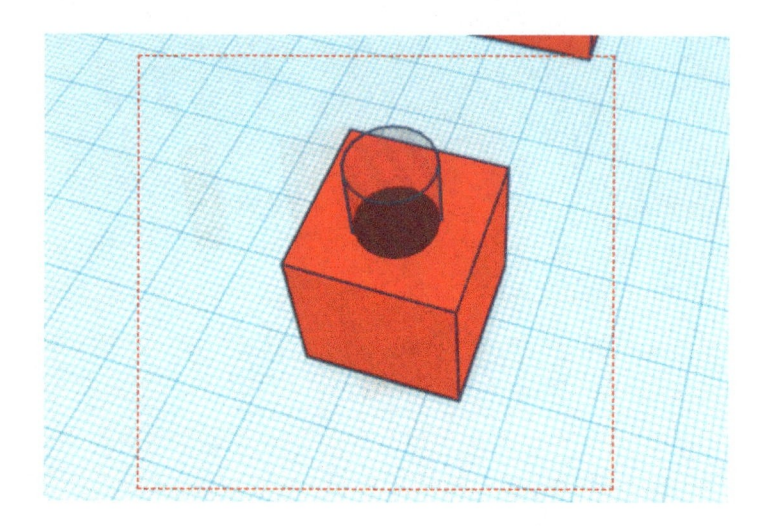

Thereafter, the tools in the bar on the top right are released for editing, and we can select "Group". Think about what's going to happen now beforehand, maybe you'll figure it out. (Note: The cylinder is a negative, subtractive element).

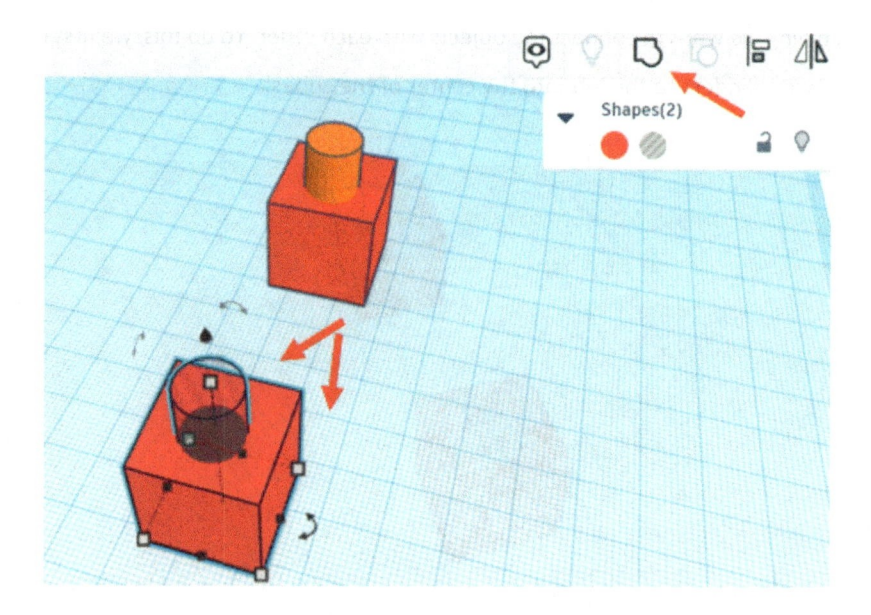

As a result, the following new object is created:

34

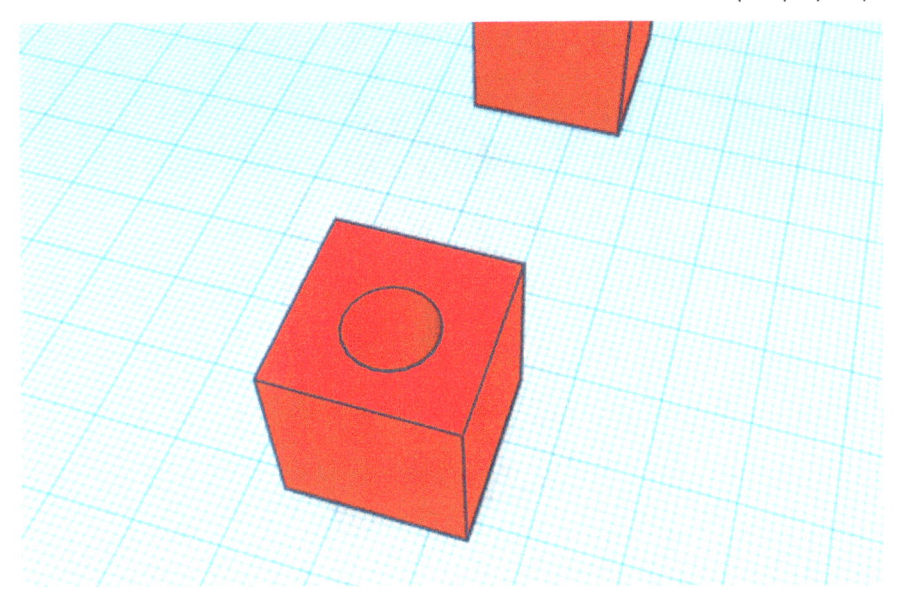

It is a cube with a hole in the middle. The hole came about because we subtracted the negative (subtractive) element, which is the cylinder, from the positive element, which is the cube. Excellent, if you figured it out. If not, it doesn't matter, just keep reading, your spatial imagination will be trained more and more throughout the book. Try to imagine it spatially like this: If you want to drill a hole in the analog world, take a drill bit that has a basic cylindrical shape and the diameter of the hole you plan to make. When you drill a hole, you basically do nothing else than inserting a cylindrical object (drill) into another component to create a hole. The drill is the subtracting, negative element.

What will happen now if we connect or group the other two objects (cube and "solid" cylinder)? Please think about it for a moment, and only then take a look at the next page. (Note: The cylinder in this case is an additive, adding element). The procedure is identical.

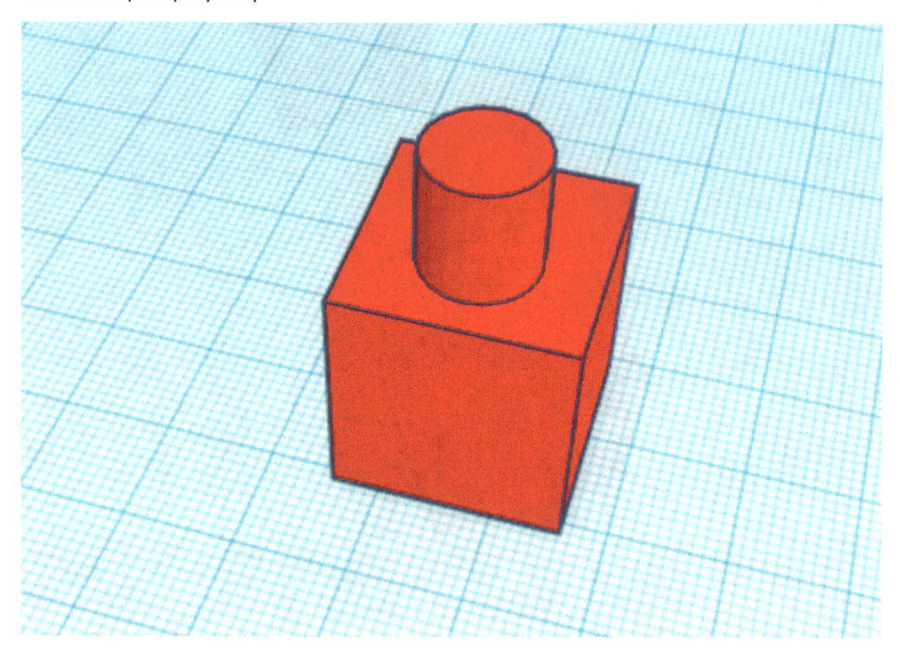

A fused, solid body is created. The color of the cylinder is also matched to the base body, since it is now a common body. Great, if that's how you imagined it. So now we know the difference between "solid" and "hole" and we have already learned an essential function ("Group") for further construction. With "Ungroup" you can undo this merging process. To do this, simply select the objects that you want to separate again and then choose " Ungroup". You can also select several objects at once. The program will then recognize the affiliations by itself.

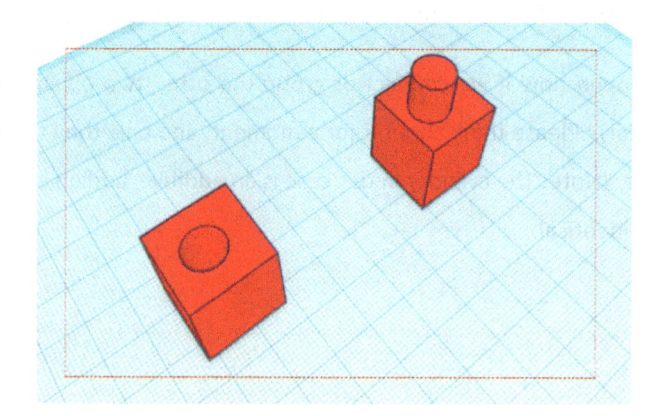

Tinkercad | Step by Step

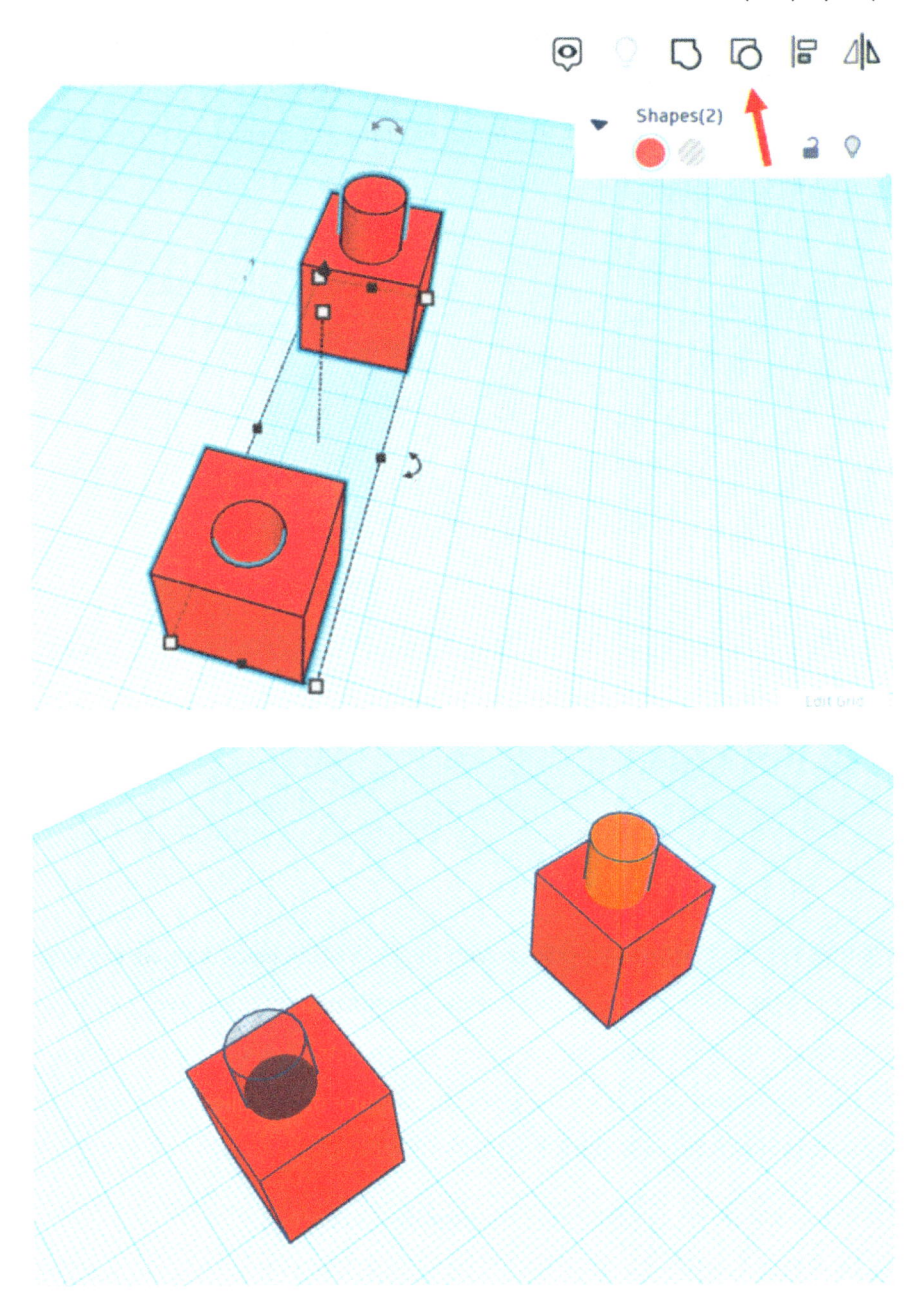

The two fusion processes are thus reversed, and we now have four independent bodies again instead of just two.

37

Tinkercad | Step by Step

With the "Align" function, you can control the alignment of two or more objects to each other. You could also just move the objects as you want them, but with "Align" this is much faster, easier and also more accurate. For example, we create two simple cylinders ("Basic Shapes") and select them both and then click on "Align".

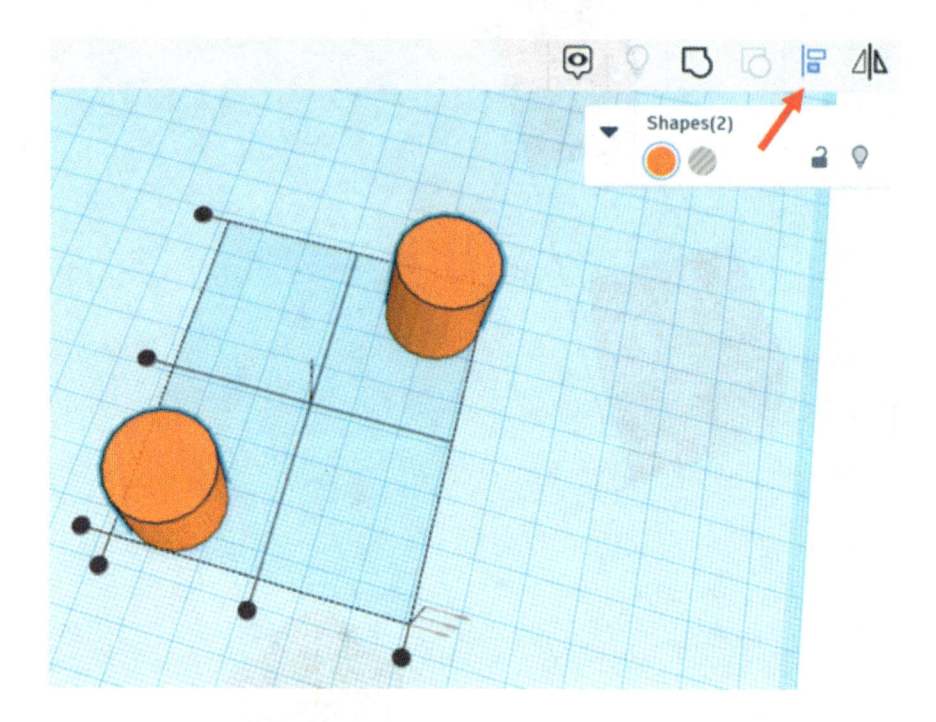

We then get a field with black points. With the help of the black dots, we can now determine the alignment of the two cylinders on the basis of the drawn lines. If we move our computer mouse over one of the black points, the alignment is displayed symbolically. When we click on the point, the alignment is applied. Have a look at the two examples below and try it out for yourself!

a) Preview before click (mouse cursor is over the red dot):

Tinkercad | Step by Step

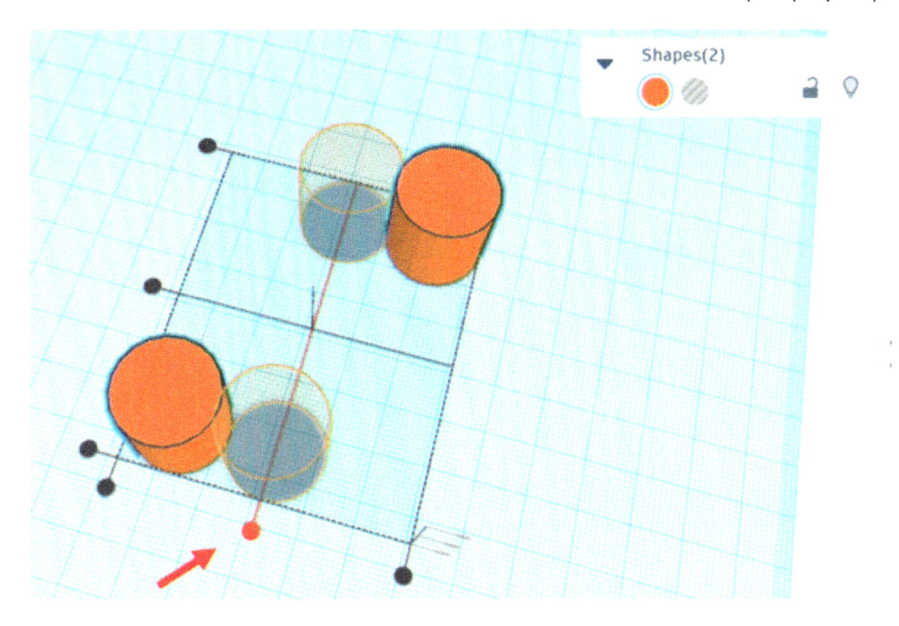

a) Result after clicking on the red dot (alignment has been performed):

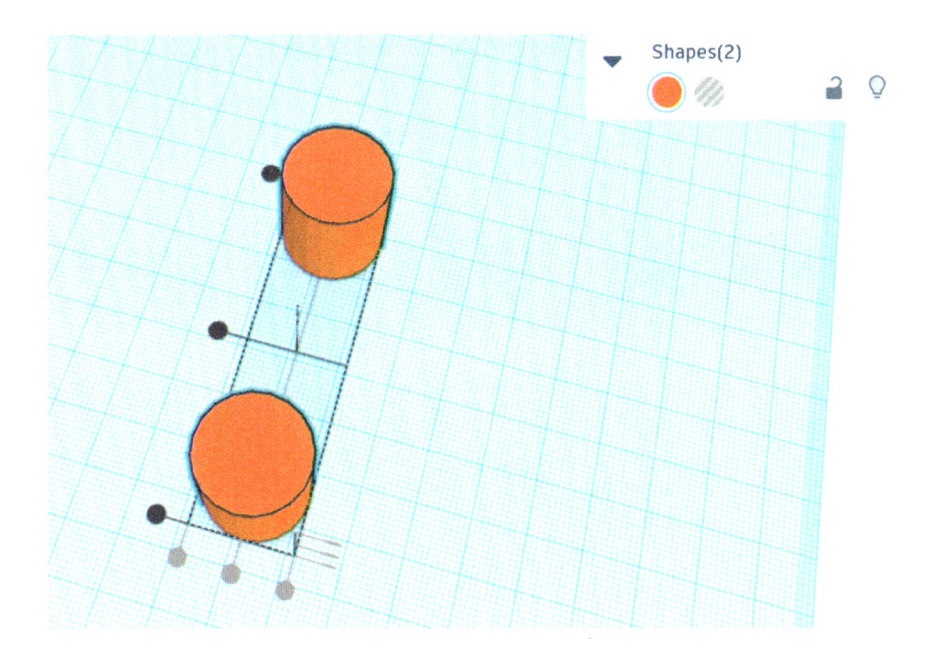

39

Tinkercad | Step by Step

b) Preview before click (mouse cursor is over the red dot):

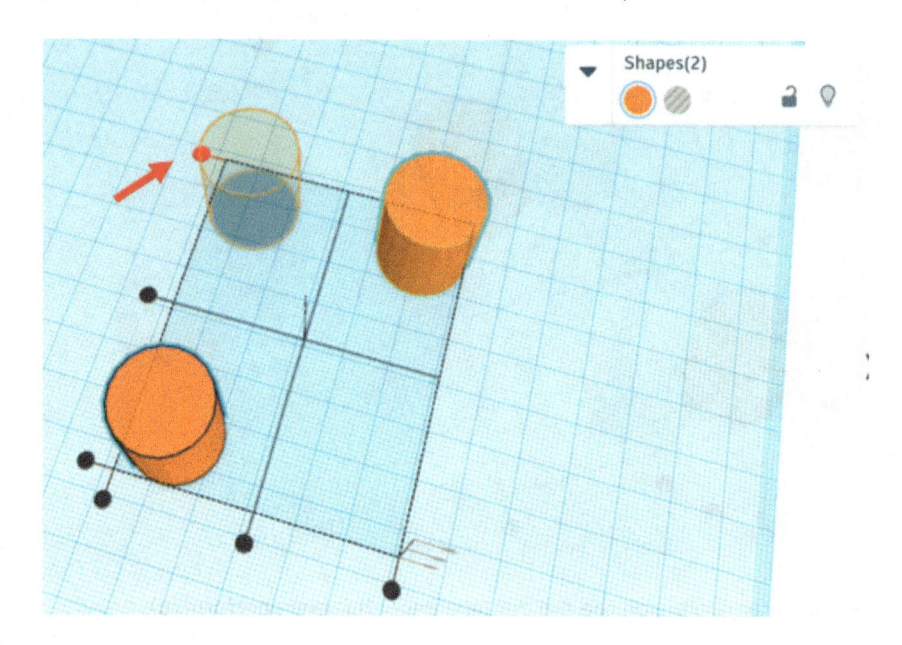

b) Result after clicking on the red dot (alignment has been performed):

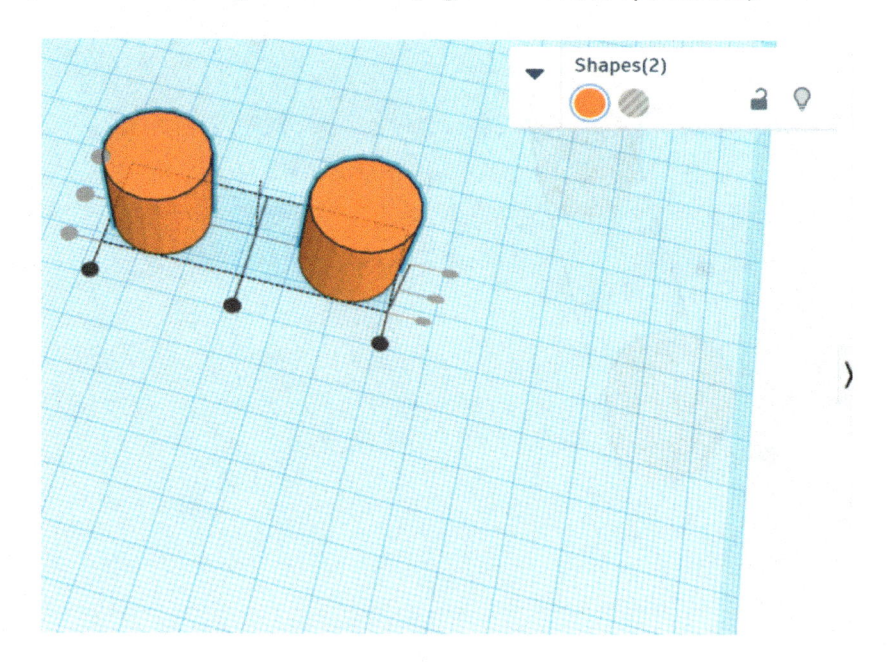

The last function we will look at here is the "Mirror" function. This allows us to mirror an object, that is, to change the orientation of the object. Let's take a look at this using a "TEXT" object.

When we select the body and the Mirror function, three small double arrows appear.

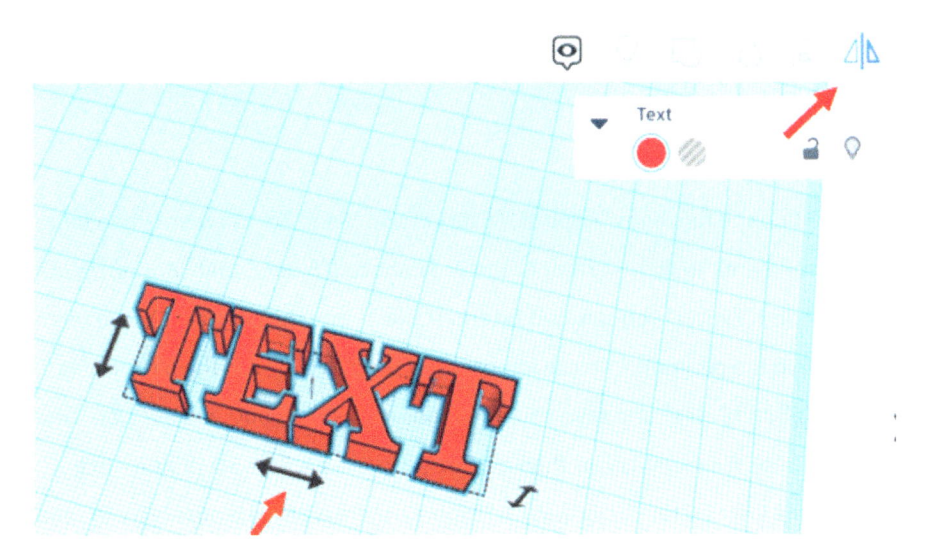

Depending on which of these arrows we now click, the object will be mirrored based on these directions. For example, if we choose the arrow that is at the bottom center, we get the following result:

Tinkercad | Step by Step

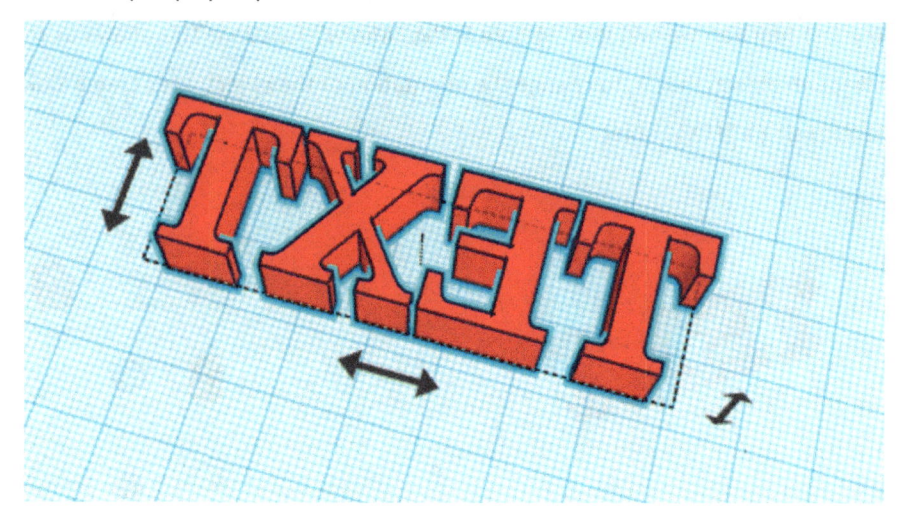

The text has now been mirrored in the sideways direction. Try out the other arrows as well, and try it out on other objects. It's best to think about what the result will look like beforehand. Before we finally close this chapter, let's take a look at the upper-right area of the environment.

Here we find the functions "Import", "Export" and "Send To", as well as two more 3D environments to choose from in the area above ("Blocks" and "Bricks"). With "Import" and "Export" you can load external objects into the program or save them from within the program. You can import objects up to 25 MB in the file formats ". stl", ". obj" and ". svg" and save your creations as ". stl", ". obj" and as ". glb" and ". svg". These file formats can then be further processed for 3D printing (e.g., ". stl") or for a laser cutter (". svg"). With "Export", there is also the possibility to send the file directly to your connected 3D printer. If you are also interested in 3D printing, take a look at my course on it (information on the last pages).

Tinkercad | Step by Step

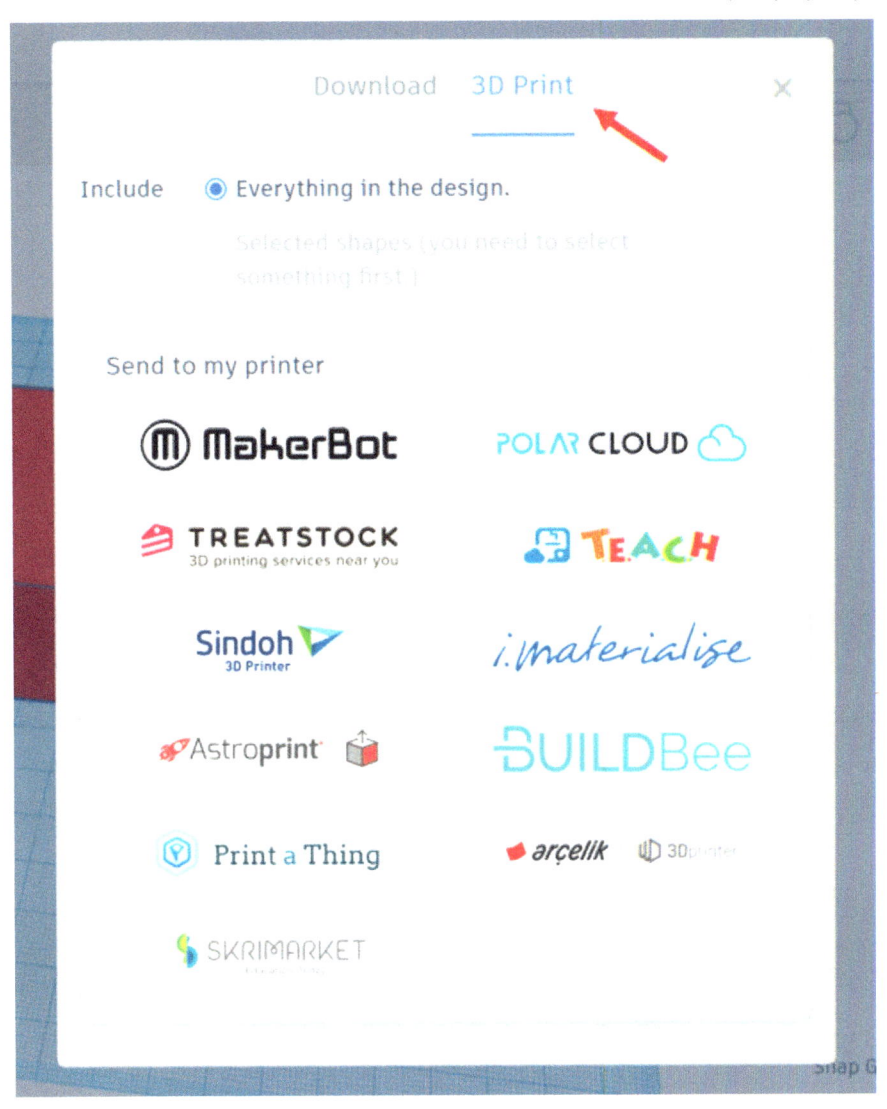

With "Send to" you can also send a file of your object via email or to other platforms, such as "Thingiverse" or "MyMiniFactory". Here there is also the option to further edit the file in Fusion 360.

43

Tinkercad | Step by Step

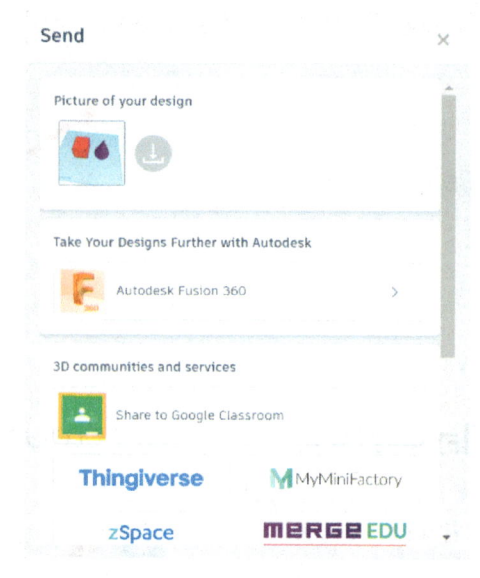

In Tinkercad, there is the possibility to display your designs in other environments. For this purpose, you have the possibility to display your objects in "Blocks", as building blocks, or in "Bricks", as clamping blocks. This can be helpful if you want to rebuild your designs in real life instead of printing them out.

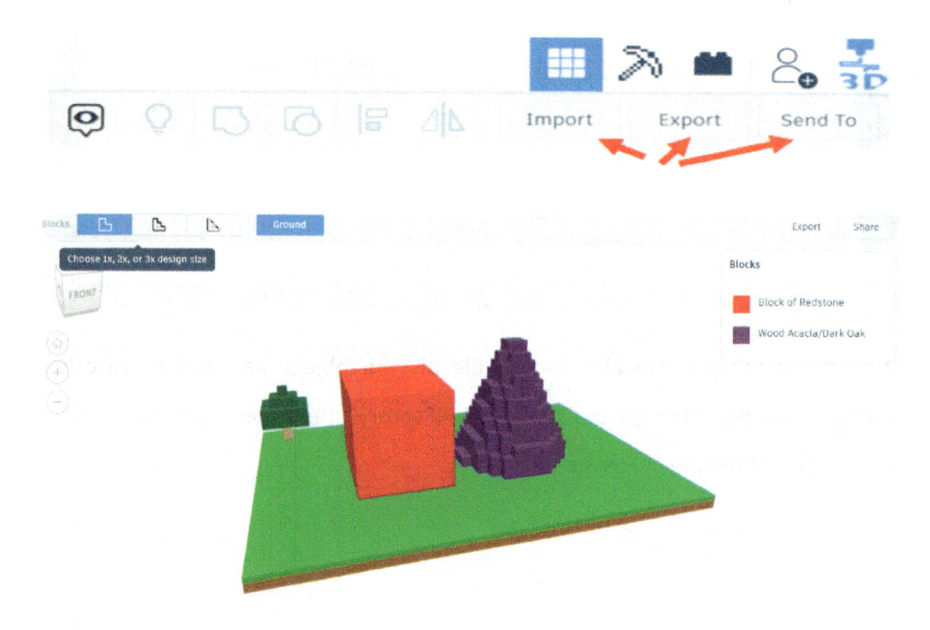

44

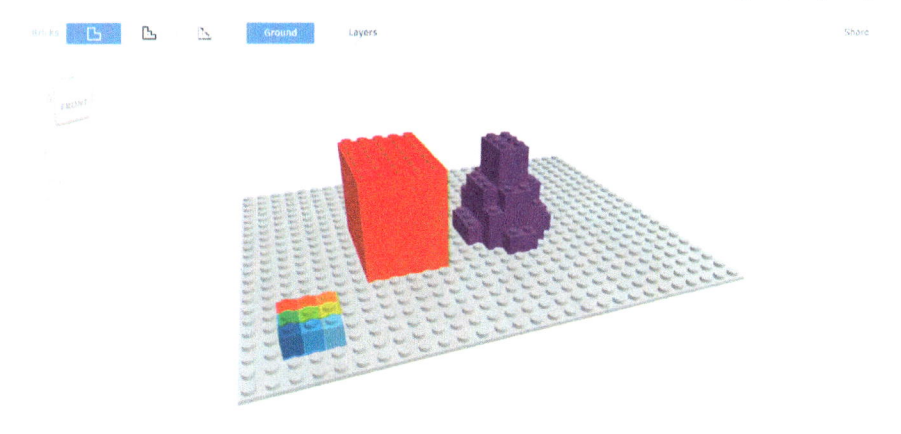

At the top left, you can find settings for the design size and the display. Just try it out!

Excellent! Now we already know our way around the 3D design environment very well, and we can start designing sample projects in the following chapters. First, we will create a smartphone case. We'll look at how this works step by step. We could then even print this out with a 3D printer and use it.

3.3 CAD project 1: Smartphone cover

For the smartphone case, we start a new project with "+ New" and "3D Design" on the start page of Tinkercad. We then simply name it smartphone case, for example. We can do that on the top left. Just click on it and rename it.

Now, how could we construct such a smartphone case?

45

Tinkercad | Step by Step

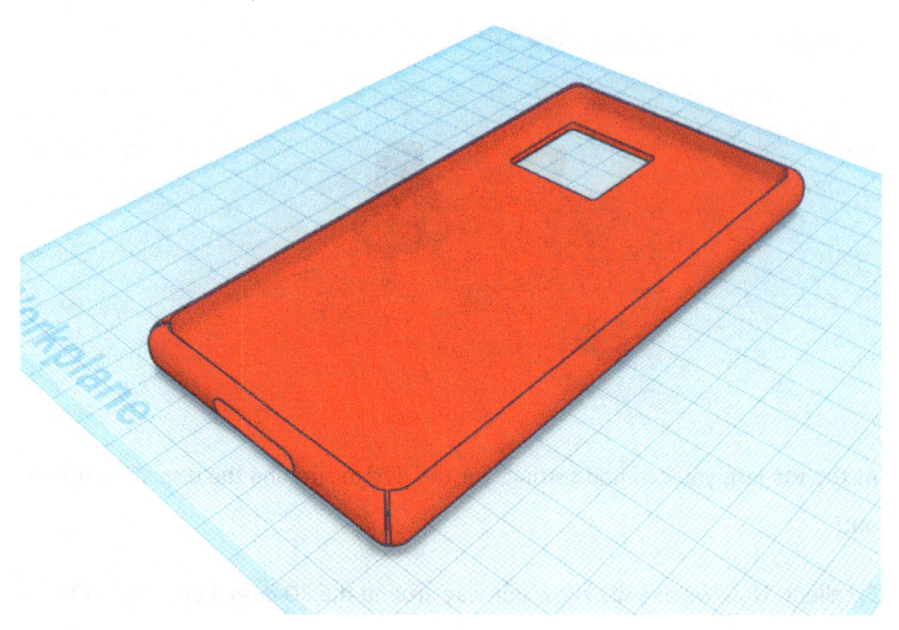

We will first create a basic body for this, which we will make exactly 2 mm larger than our smartphone is. We can either find the dimensions for this on the Internet or we can simply measure our phone ourselves (length, width, and height). We will create the basic body with a cube ("Basic Shapes").

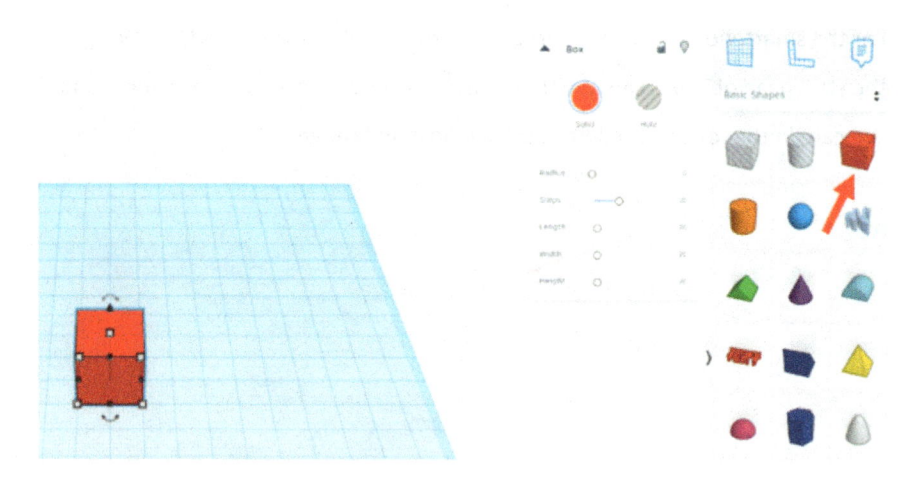

We can now enter the dimensions of our smartphone (+ 2 mm) in the settings. We will find out why we need 2 mm more in a moment. For example, my smartphone

Tinkercad | Step by Step

has the dimensions 150 mm x 75 mm x 9.5 mm (LxWxH). So, my base body needs to be 152 mm long, 77 mm wide and 11.5 mm high. If you click on the number to the right of the sliders, you can also enter the number right away and don't have to play with the setting sliders.

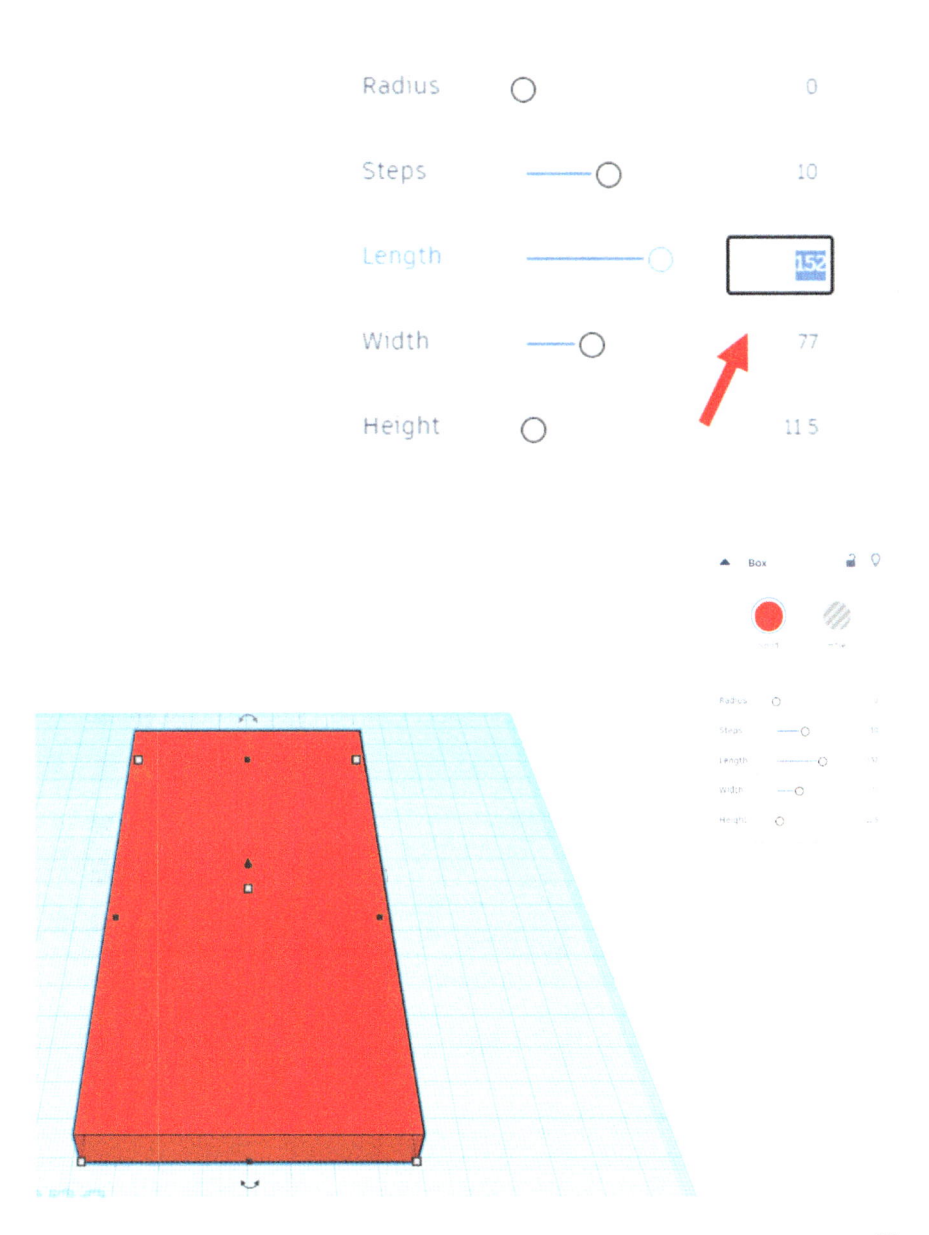

Tinkercad | Step by Step

Now we need an opening in which we can put the smartphone. That means we have to hollow out the solid base body. Can you imagine how we do that?

That's right, we simply subtract a body that is the size of our smartphone (i.e., 2 mm smaller than the base body), thus obtaining a shell with 1 mm wall thickness or thickness. That is, we create a negative body ("hole") with dimensions 150 mm x 75 mm (or with your smartphone dimensions). We set the height to 15 mm, for example. We will find out why in a moment.

If we want to print and use the cover with a 3D printer, we should subtract 1-2 mm from these dimensions so that the smartphone fits tightly, and the cover does not get lost. Depending on the 3D printer and settings, you may have to play around with this value a bit to get the perfect fit for your smartphone.

So, we'll just go with the actual dimensions for the smartphone. For the height, however, we choose the 15 mm instead of 9.5 mm, since the negative object should be a bit higher than the red base body to get an opening at the top.

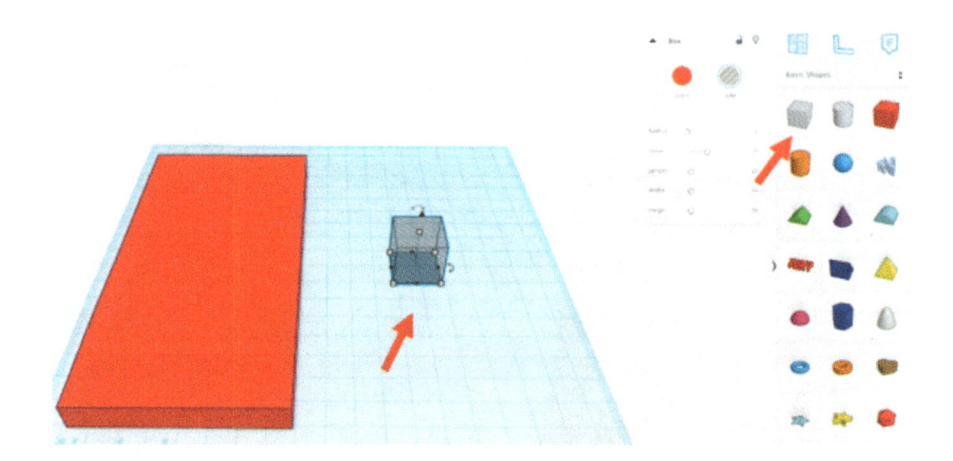

48

Tinkercad | Step by Step

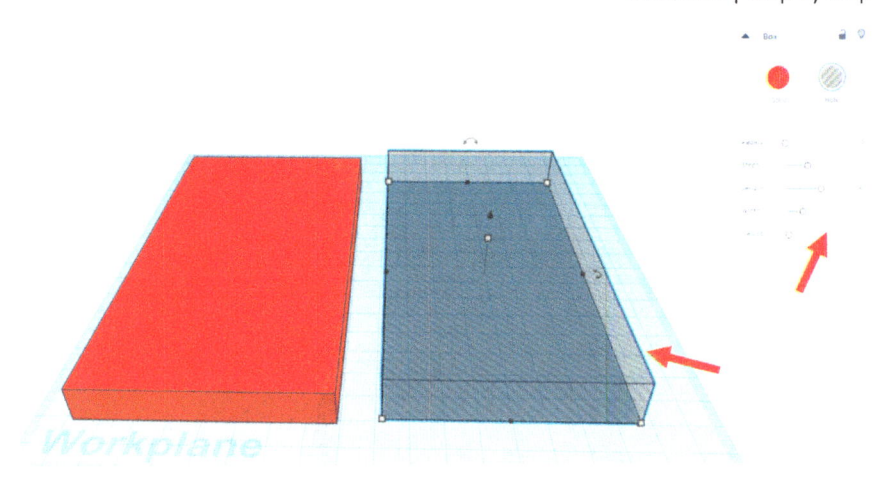

Next, we have to bring the two bodies congruently on top of each other. We can do this either by moving them or, since we need to be exactly centered, by using the "Align" function we have already learned. To do this, first select both bodies with the left mouse button pressed and a dragging motion (red rectangle must appear) and then select the function at the top right.

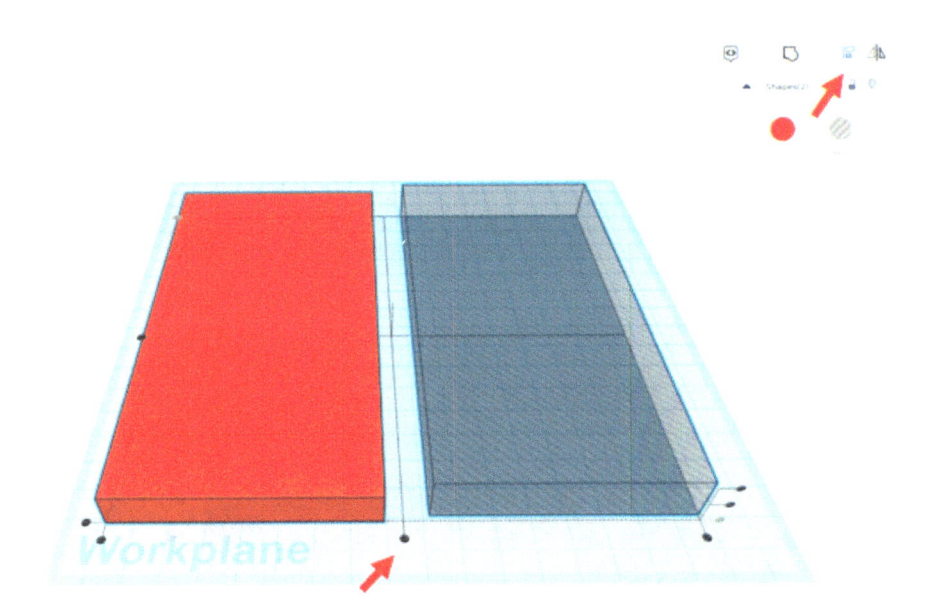

49

Tinkercad | Step by Step

Now the black points for alignment appear. We need to select the lower, middle point so that we get a congruent alignment based on the center line.

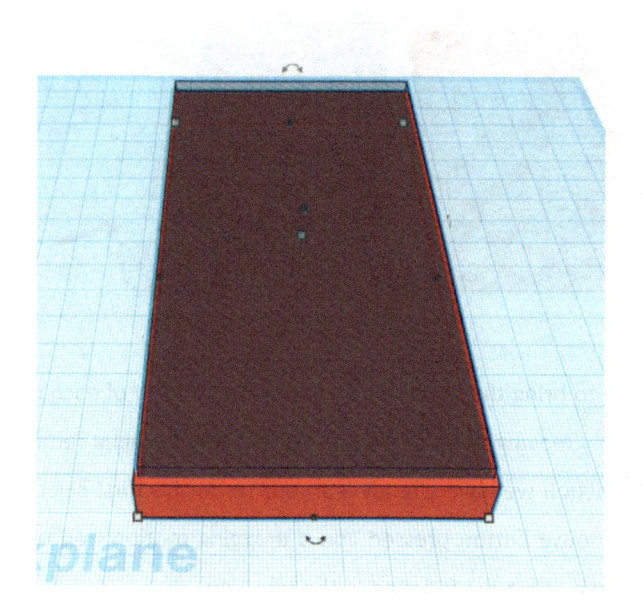

The alignment in the first direction (horizontal or horizontal x-direction, if we consider the work plane to be a two-dimensional coordinate system) is now correct. But if we set the view with the view cube on the top left to "left", we see that the distance in the back area is much smaller compared to the front area, so it is still not correct.

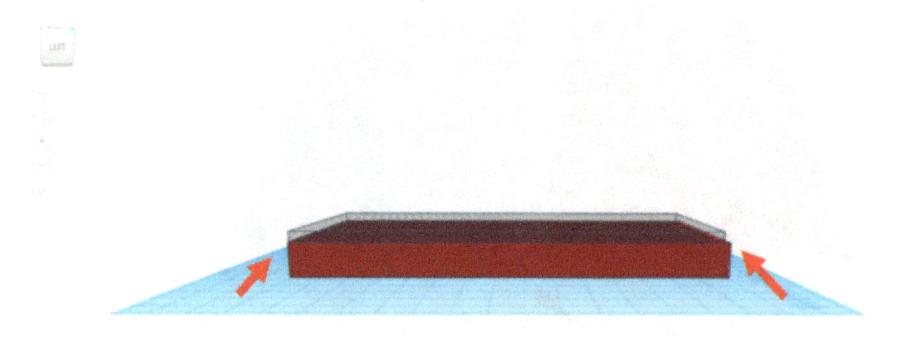

Tinkercad | Step by Step

We must therefore select both bodies again, select the "Align" function and also select the left center black point for the correct, second alignment (vertical or vertical y-direction). Then our negative body and the base body are aligned centered to each other.

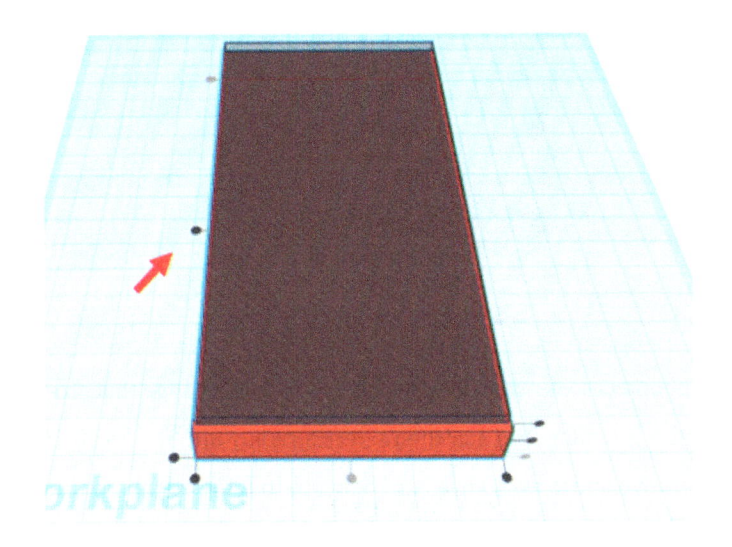

Perfect! Before we group the two bodies to make the cutout for the smartphone, we still have to move the negative body ("hole") up by 1 mm so that a base area of the base body remains. Otherwise, we would only get a frame. You are welcome to try both for better understanding. We do the shifting by dragging the small gray arrow, which is in the middle of the body when it is selected, upwards by exactly 1 mm.

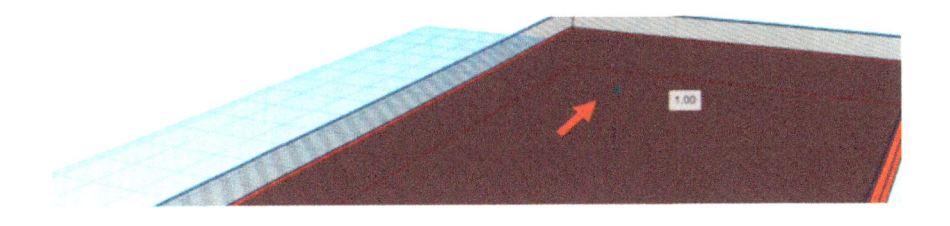

Then we can select and group both shapes and in this way, we get the basic shape of our smartphone case with 1 mm wall thickness.

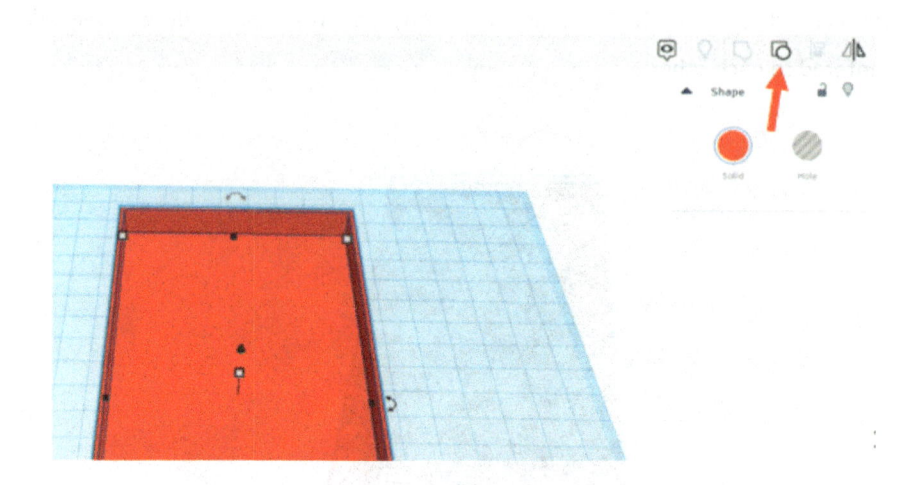

The smartphone case is now still very angular, we will change that. To do this, we first undo the grouping. We can then select a radius of 5 mm in the settings for both the positive and the negative base body, so that the edges are rounded. First, we do this for the red base body.

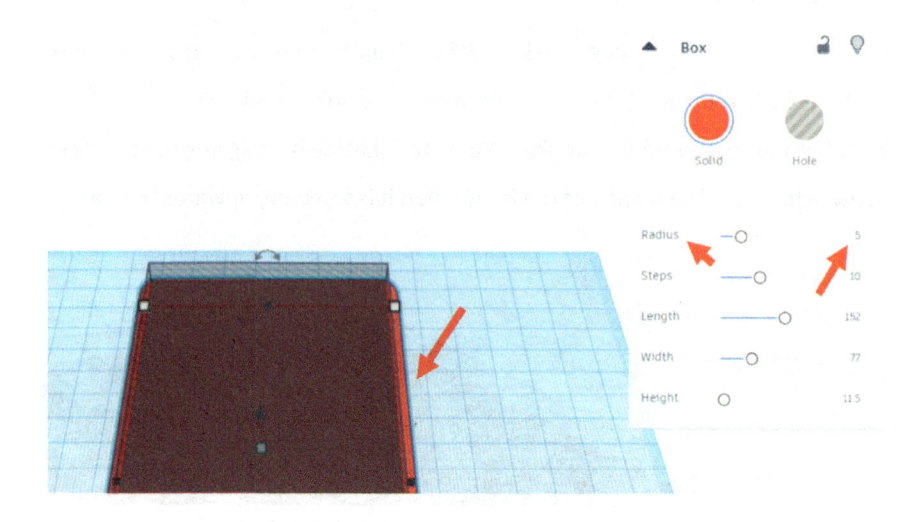

Then we do the same for the negative body, through which we then get our clipping.

Tinkercad | Step by Step

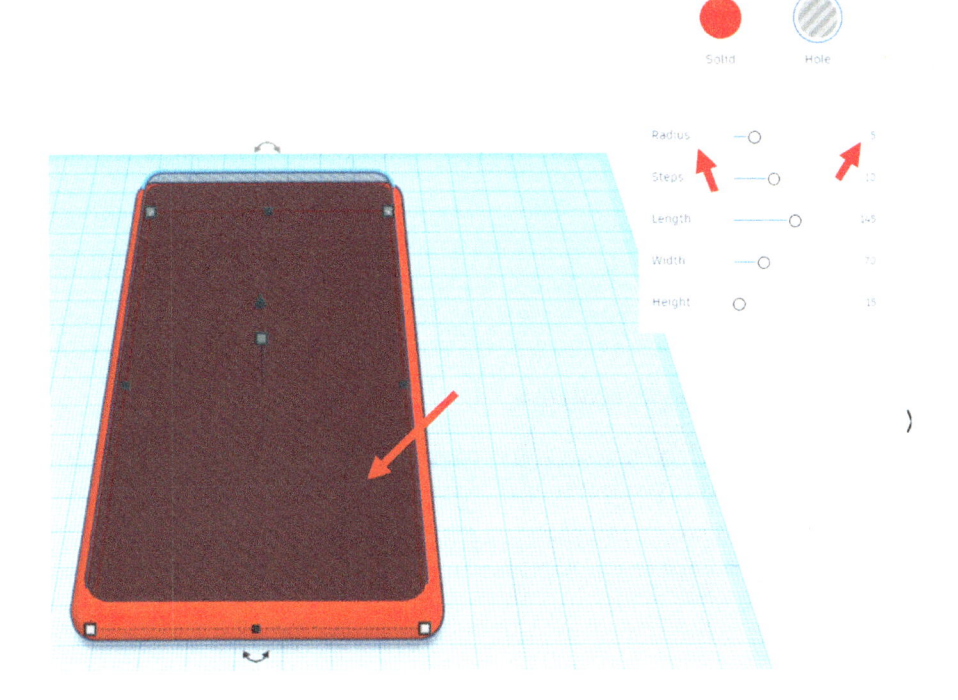

After grouping the two solids again, we get the following shape for our smartphone case:

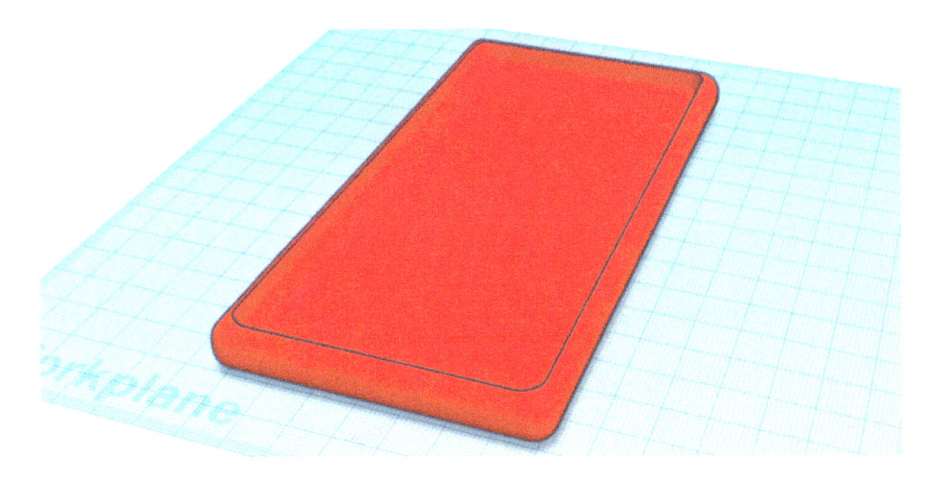

Then we create a few openings for the camera on the back, as well as for connections at the bottom front. The procedure for this is again identical. We

53

Tinkercad | Step by Step

create a new negative body ("hole") and subtract it from the base body to create an opening. Let's try this for the opening for the camera on the back. For example, we will create a negative body for the camera module with the dimensions 30 mm x 30 mm (L x W) and 4 mm height. We also want a radius of 20 mm so that the edges are rounded.

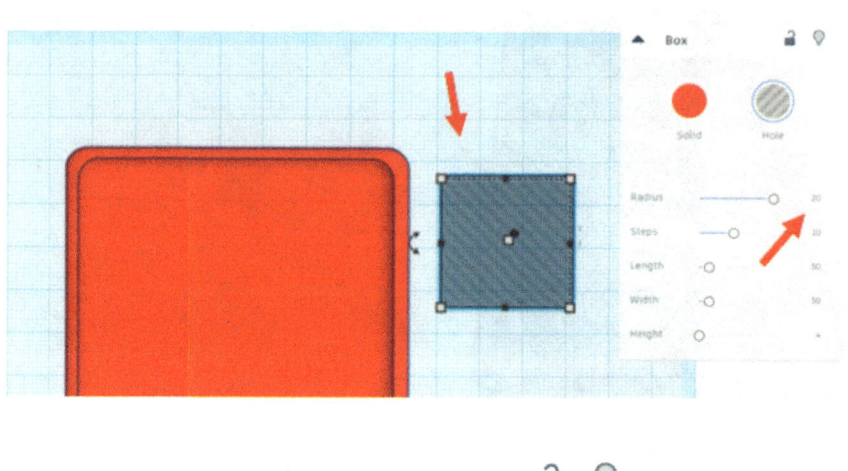

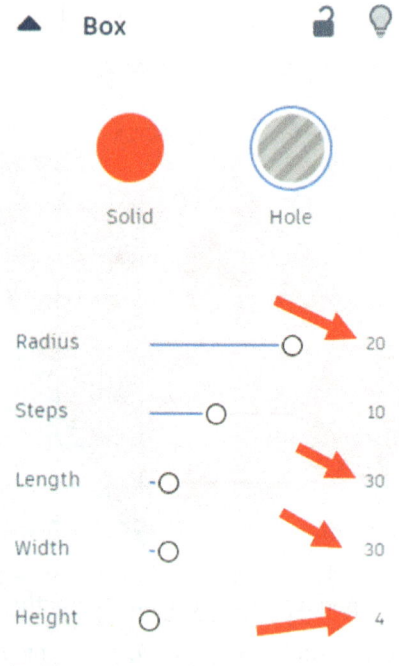

54

Tinkercad | Step by Step

In the next step, we place the negative body in the right place (for dimensions, see the smartphone) and group the two bodies so that a cutout is created. We can also use the "Ruler tool" for the placement, e.g., in the upper left corner, so that the positioning is easier when we have measured the dimensions on the smartphone.

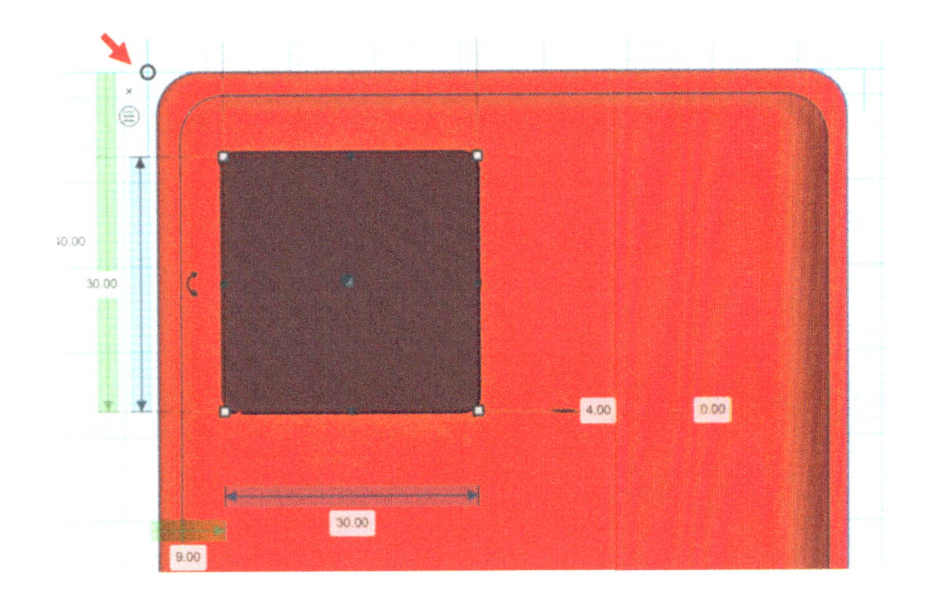

Then we move the negative body down by 1 mm so that the curves are also cut out on the opposite side.

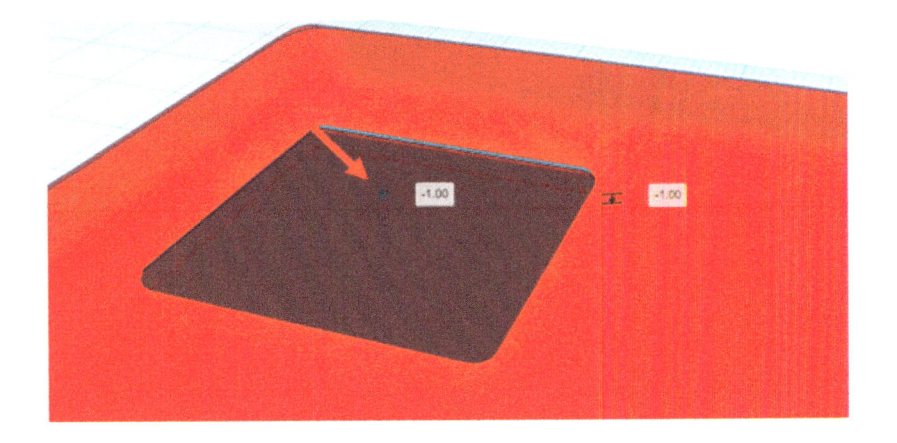

55

Tinkercad | Step by Step

After grouping the two bodies, we then get a shell that already looks very good. For the cutout for the connections in the lower area, we then again create a negative body. This should have 25 mm x 5 mm x 10 mm. Then turn the body with the small arrows so that it can be placed as shown. The placement is done with the function "Align". To do this, select both bodies and use the points shown to adjust the alignment correctly.

Tinkercad | Step by Step

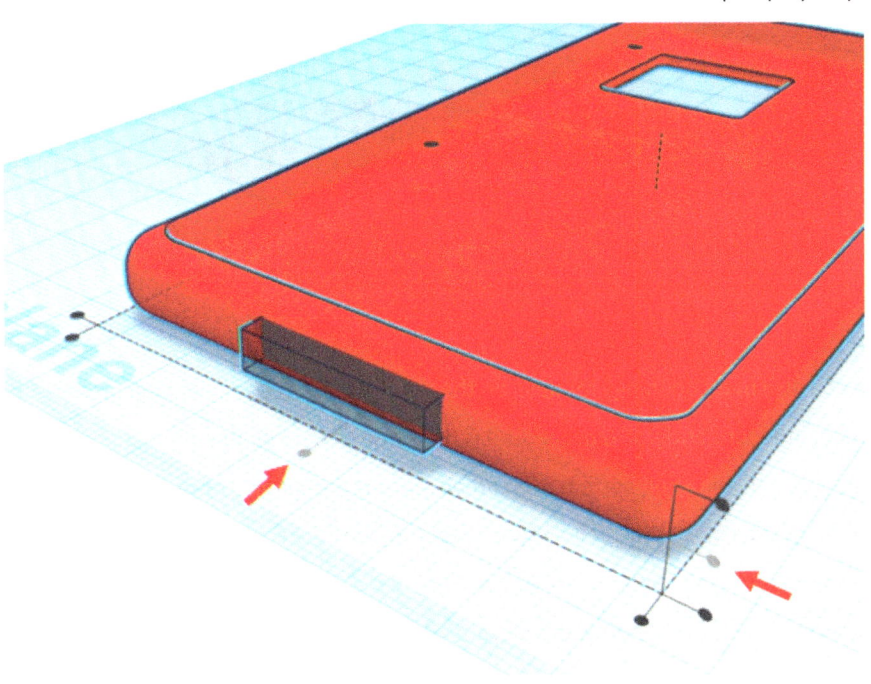

Then we give the rectangular body another 5 mm radius so that this opening is also filleted. Finally, the bodies are fused again.

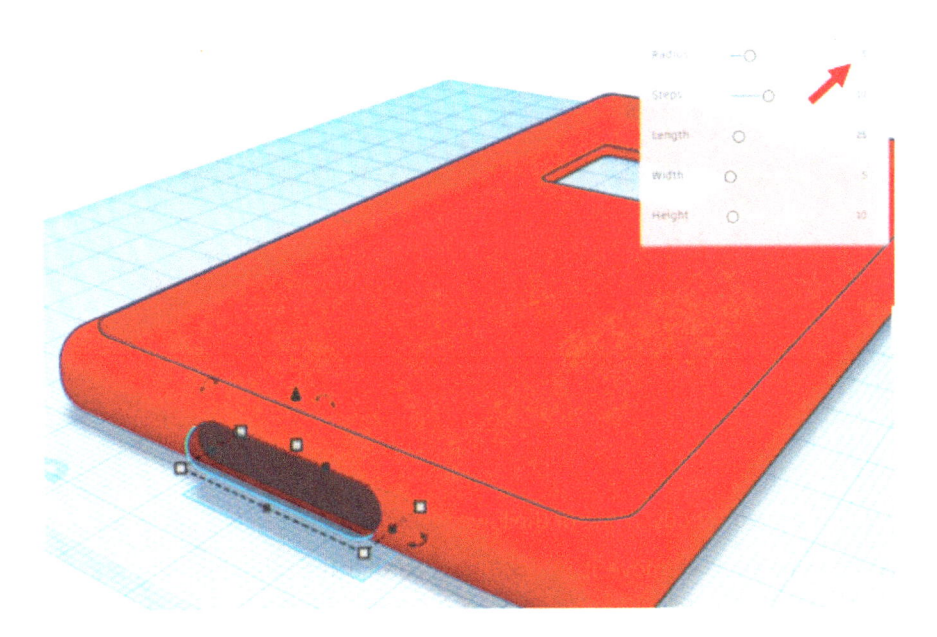

57

Tinkercad | Step by Step

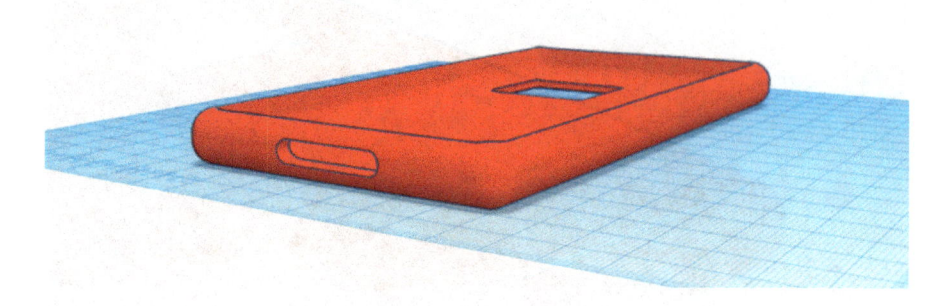

If you also need openings for keys on the right or left side, you are welcome to add them independently. The procedure is the same as before. We now add two small openings to the shell so that we can also insert the phone because for this, the shell must be able to stretch a little. To do this, we again create a small rectangular element that we rotate by -45° in the work plane (using the small rotation arrow). The dimensions of the body are 10 mm x 1 mm x 15 mm (LxWxH).

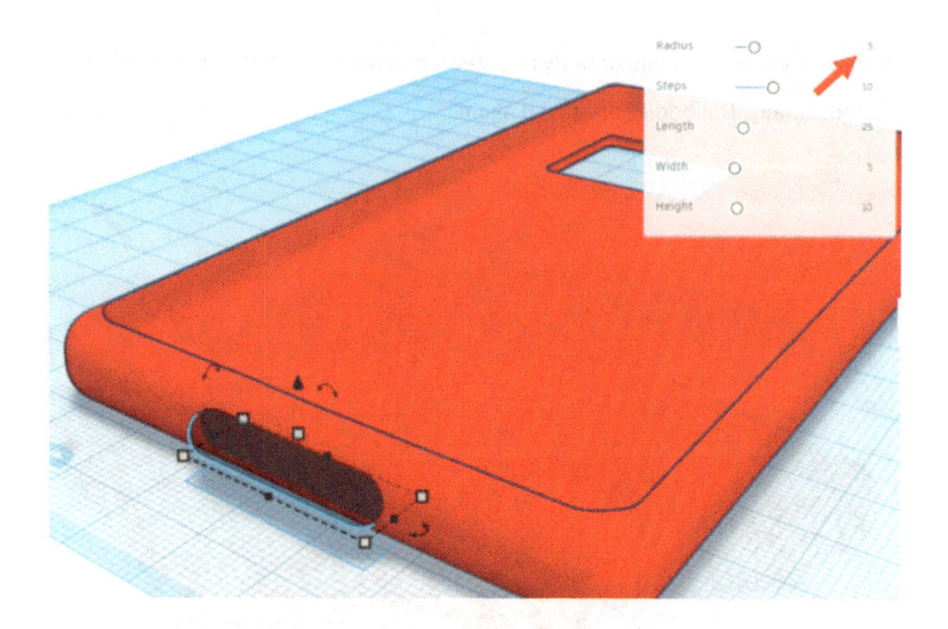

We now place this body in one of the lower corners of the envelope, as shown, and in the same step we move it up by 3 mm, so that the following indentation is created after the grouping.

58

Tinkercad | Step by Step

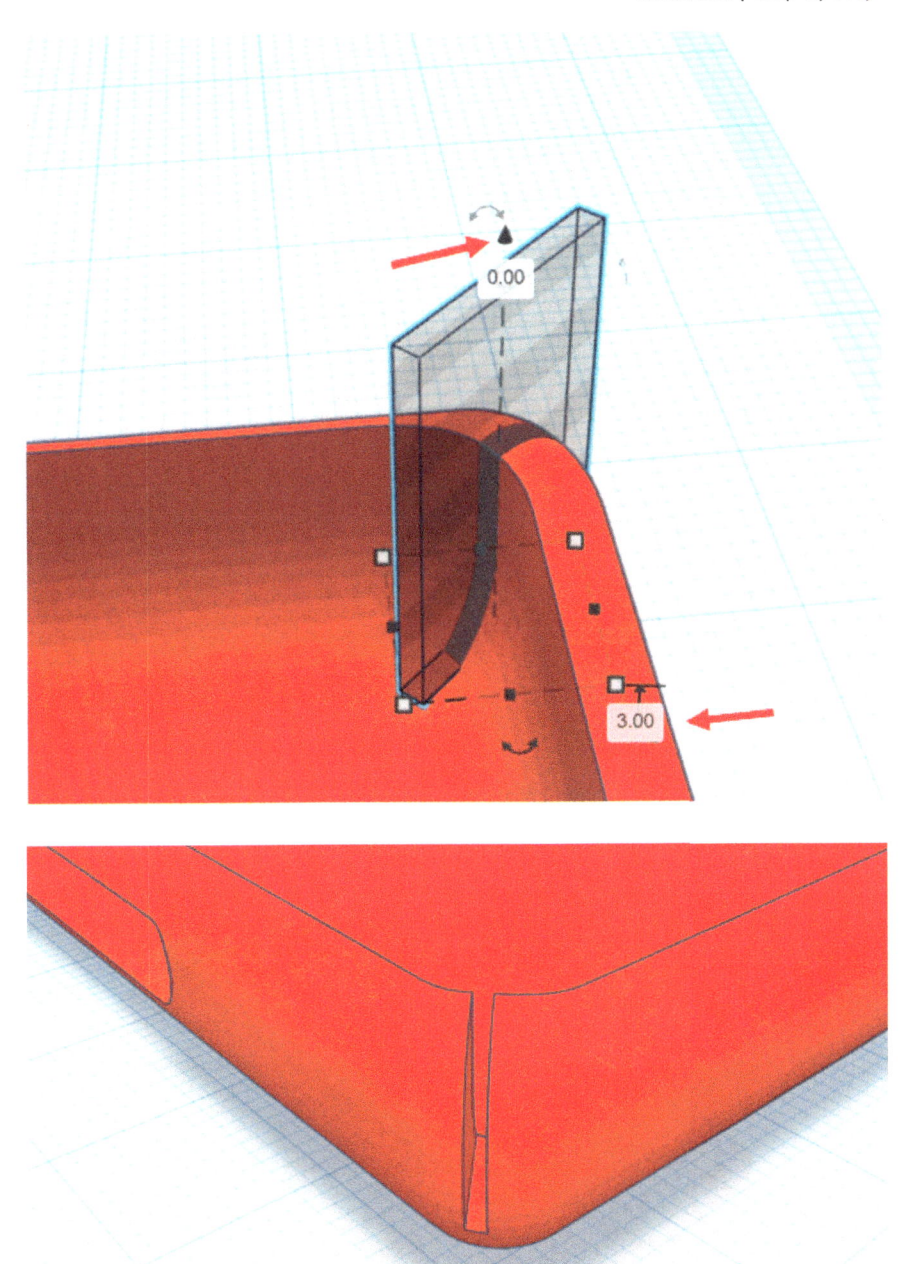

We do the same on the other side, with identical procedures.

59

Tinkercad | Step by Step

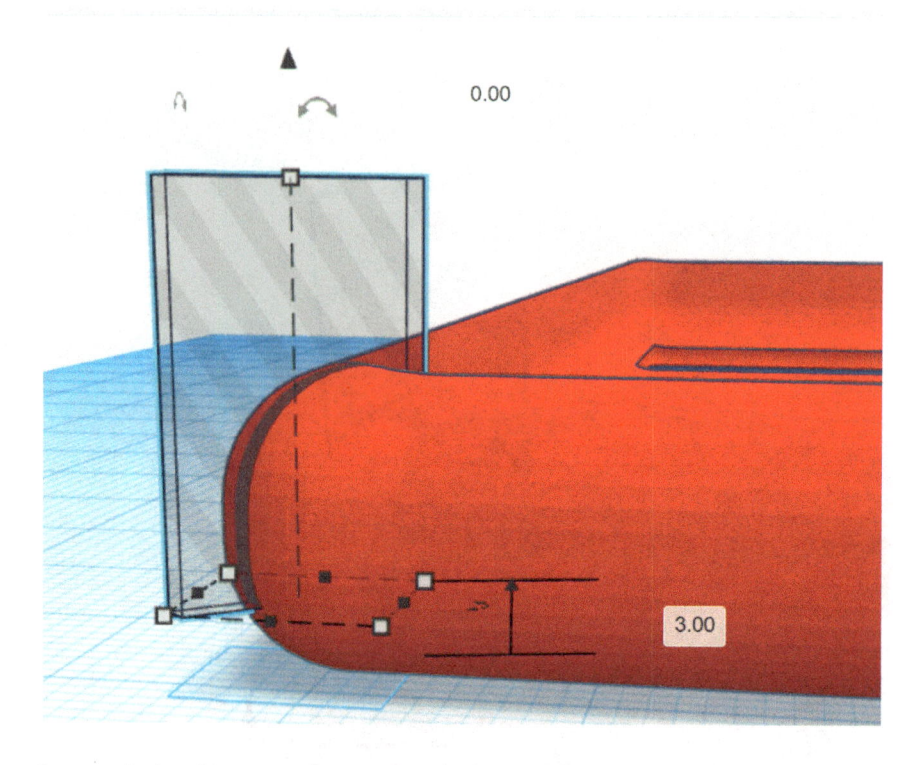

Congratulations! Now you have created a beautiful smartphone case. By the way, we don't need to save, Tinkercad does that automatically.

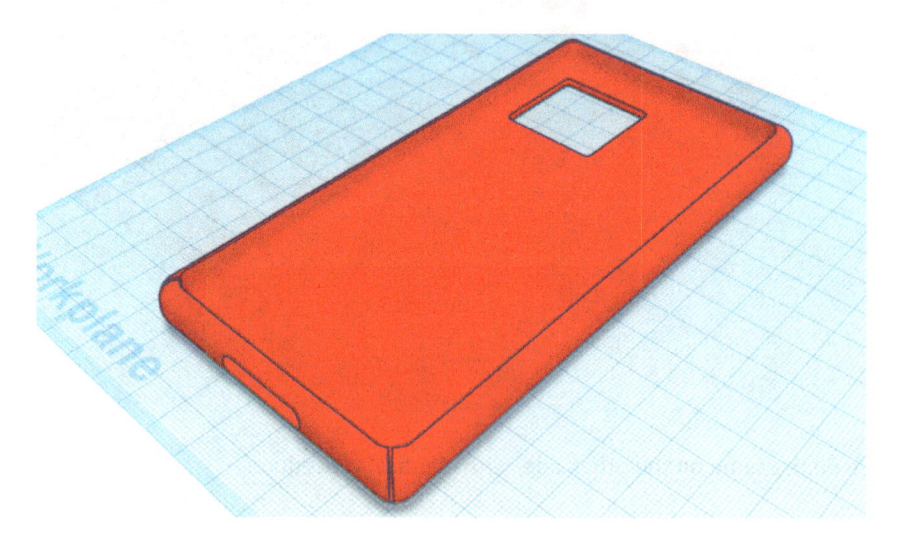

60

Tinkercad | Step by Step

3.4 CAD project 2: Wrench

We have completed our first design project. Let's continue with the second project right away!

In the following, we would like to look at how we can construct a wrench.

On the right side, we want to turn the wrench into a classic open-end wrench, while on the left side, we will create our own special tool.

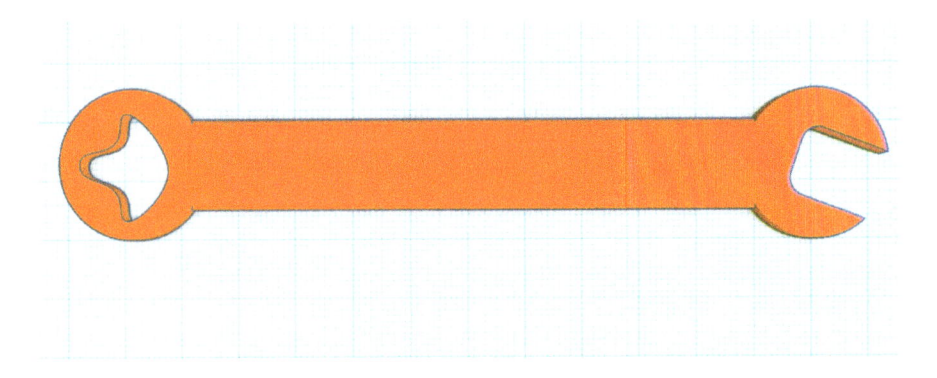

To do this, we start again with a new design and first create the center ridge of the wrench. We do this with a rectangular base body, which we dimension e.g., with 15 mm x 100 mm x 4 mm (LxWxH).

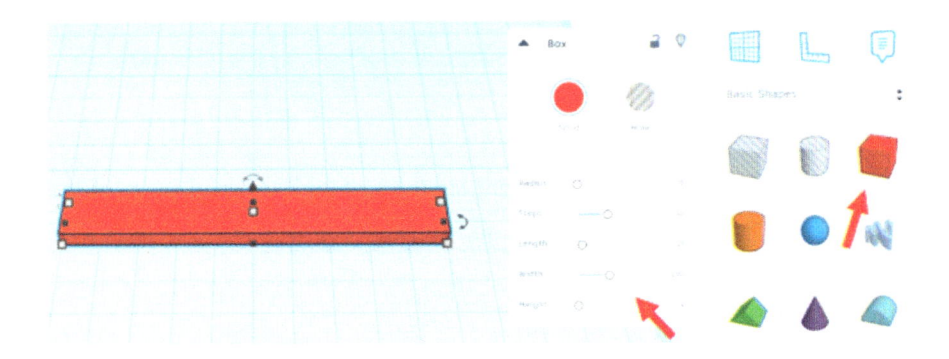

Then we create two basic cylindrical bodies for the ends of the wrench. The dimensions should be 25 x 25 mm each in the plane and 4 mm for the height. By

61

Tinkercad | Step by Step

the way, you can change the dimensions of some bodies, like the cylindrical base body here, only by dragging the small corner points.

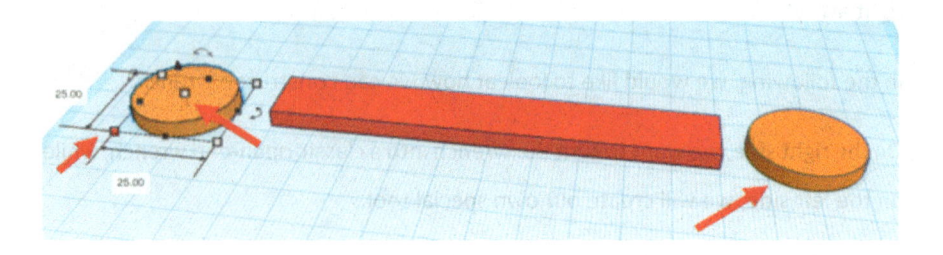

Then we move the adjustment sliders ("Sides", "Bevel", "Segments") of both cylindrical basic bodies all the way to the right, so that we get a smooth and rounded body respectively. It's best to play around with the settings, and you'll quickly understand which slider makes which change.

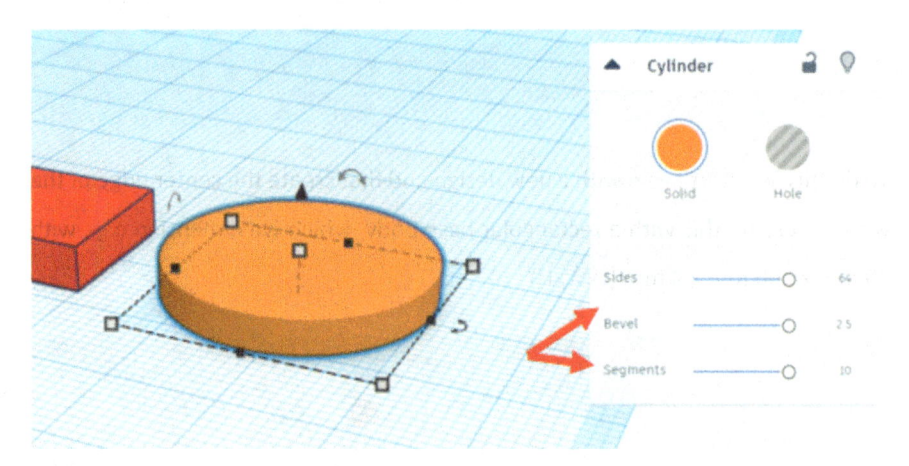

We also create another radius of 5 mm for the rectangular center piece of the wrench so that we no longer have any sharp edges.

Tinkercad | Step by Step

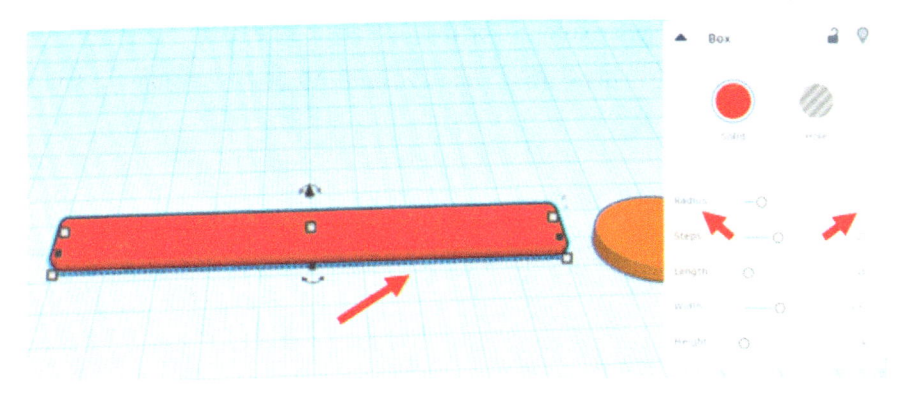

In the next step, we want to slightly overlap the two cylindrical base bodies at the ends of the centerpiece with it. To do this, we simply push them into each other a little (approximately even distance) and align all three bodies using the center line with "Align" as follows (to do this, first mark all three bodies).

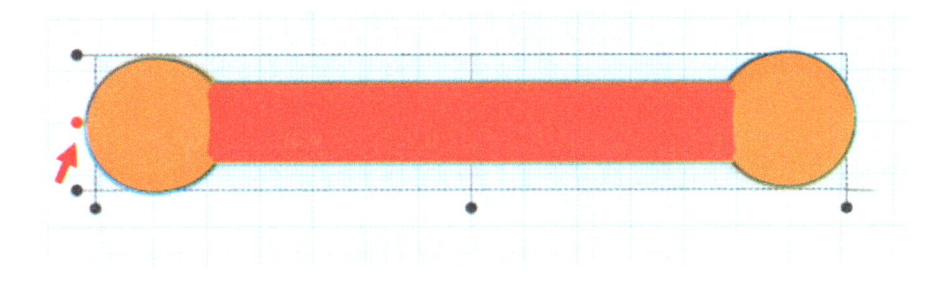

Then we merge the three bodies with the help of "Group":

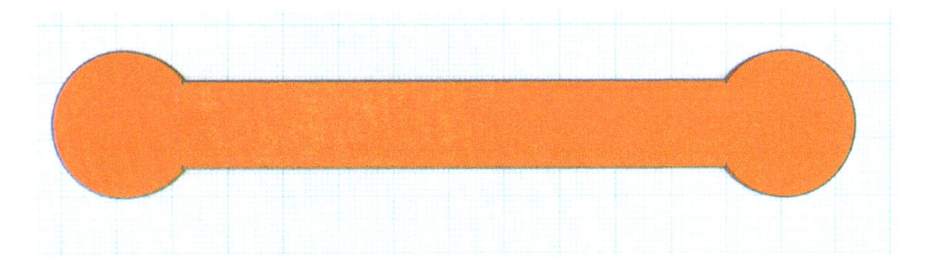

In the next step, we still need to create the openings with which we can later move the screw heads. To do this, we create a classic open-end wrench for the right side

63

Tinkercad | Step by Step

using a turned rectangular cutout. For this, we need a negative body with, for example, the following dimensions: 12 mm x 20 mm x 10 mm and a radius of 3 mm.

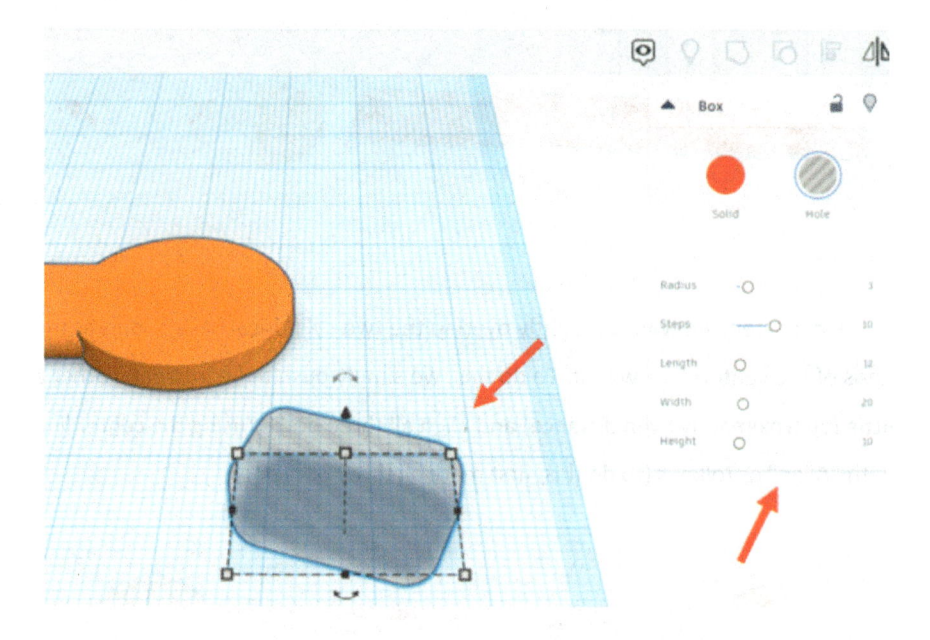

We also rotate this negative body by 20 degrees in the working plane and place it in the right area of the wrench.

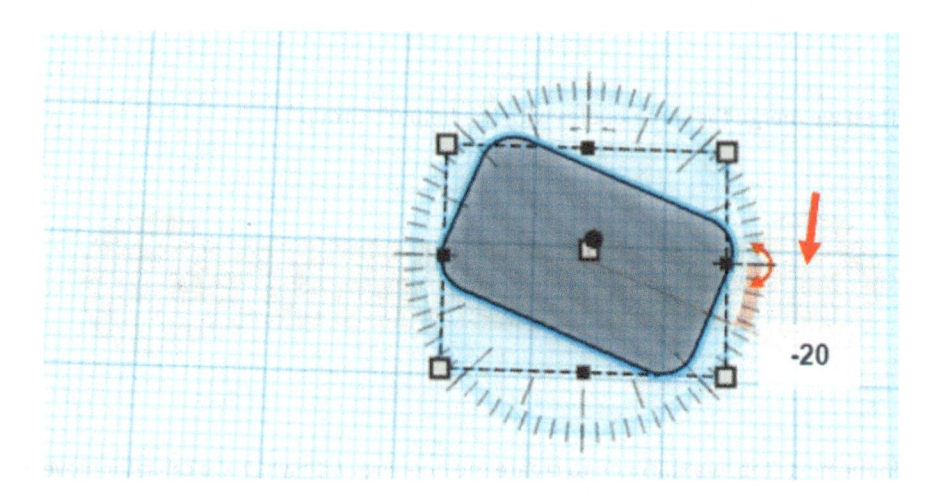

Tinkercad | Step by Step

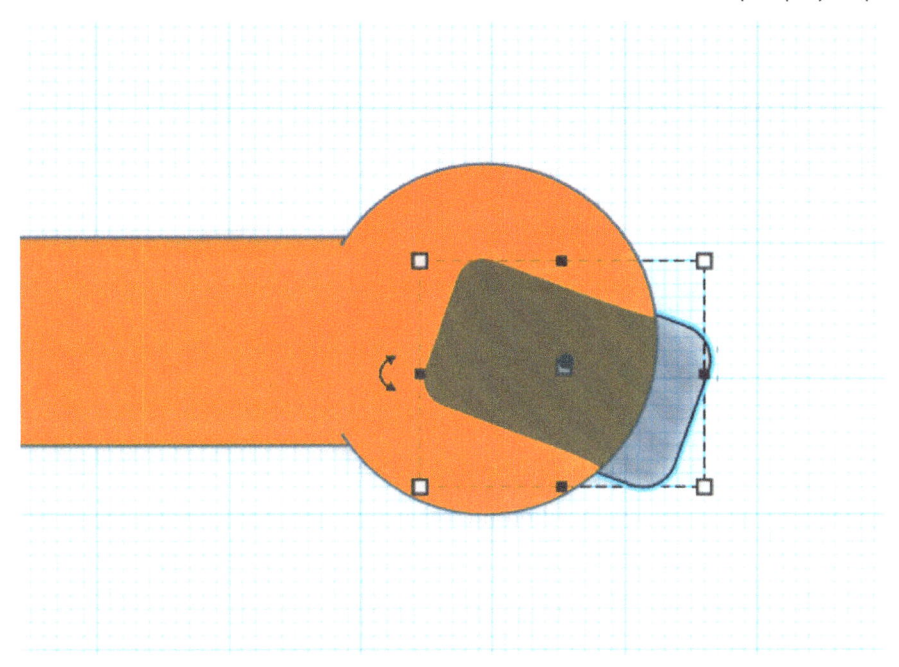

Then we need to move the cutout down by another 3 mm so that the side faces do not get any curves, but the curves only affect the back corners.

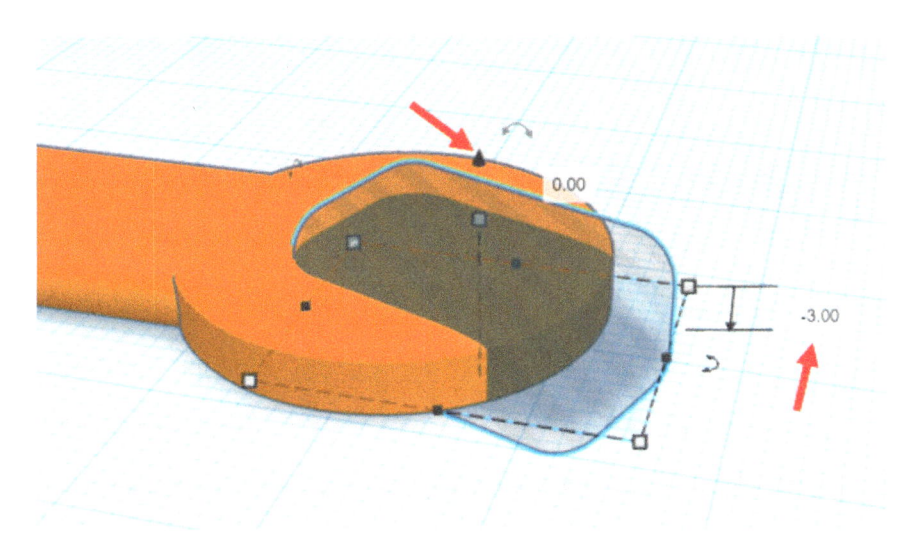

Then we can merge the bodies (Group) and thus obtain a cutout on this side of the wrench with which we can tackle a screw head.

65

Tinkercad | Step by Step

We could do the same for the other side. However, we would like to create an opening for a very special head on the other side. That's the great thing about Tinkercad, you can let your imagination run wild and create tools for exotic parts that you can't buy. For the left side of the wrench, we create an opening with a shape from the "Shape Generators" category.

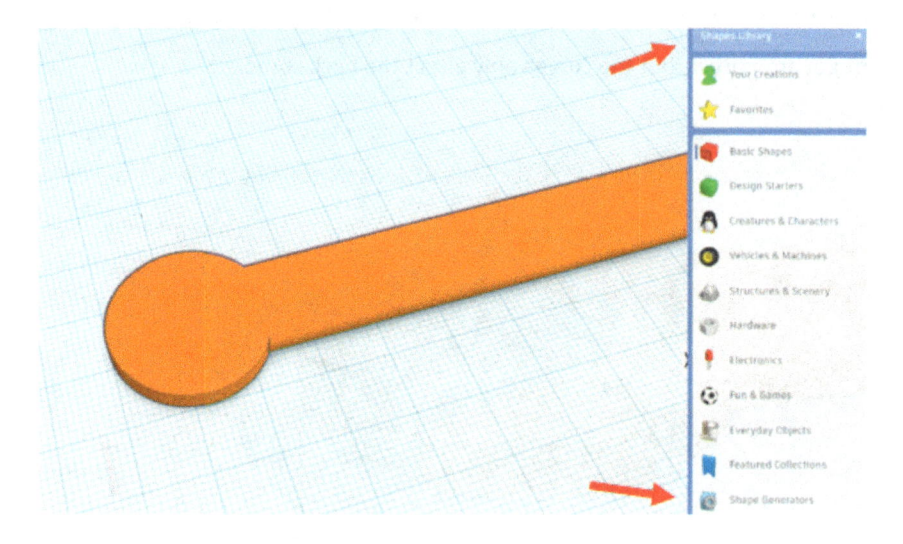

For this, we select the object "Extrusion" and switch to "Hole" because we need a cutout. For now, we just place it roughly in the left area of the wrench.

66

Tinkercad | Step by Step

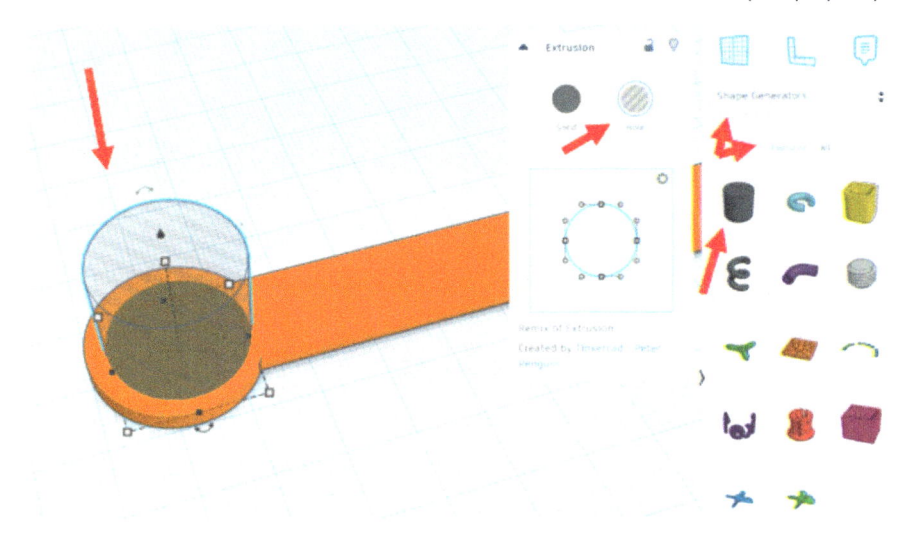

Then we can shape the object as we want. To do this, we just have to drag on the right side, in the settings window, on the points of the geometry, and we can create a shape that we need.

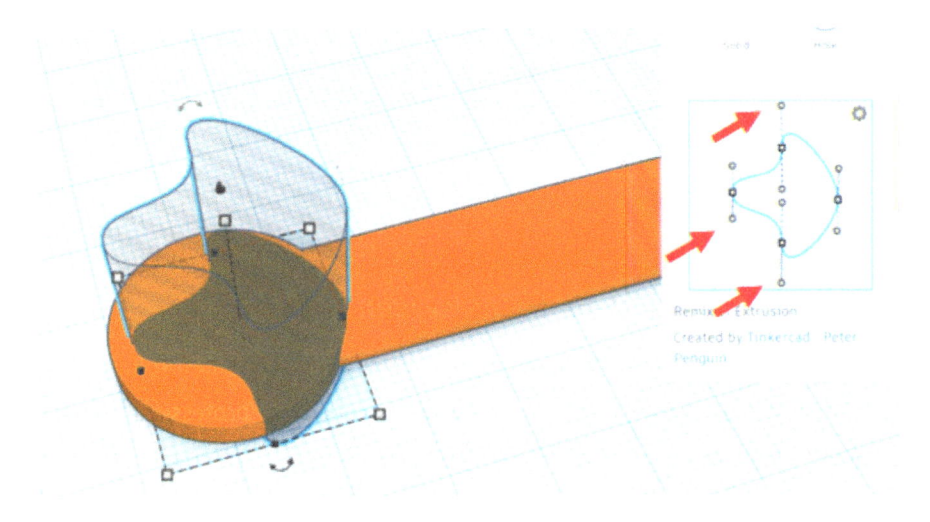

Then we can change the position and size as usual on the left side, directly on the body with the small dots and arrows.

67

Tinkercad | Step by Step

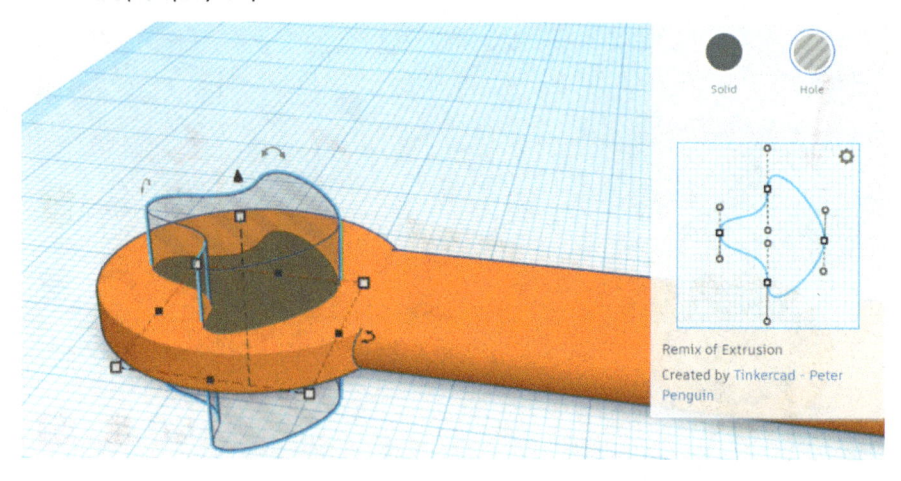

And finally, we can create the section using "Group". Now we have a special tool for our project! Excellent!

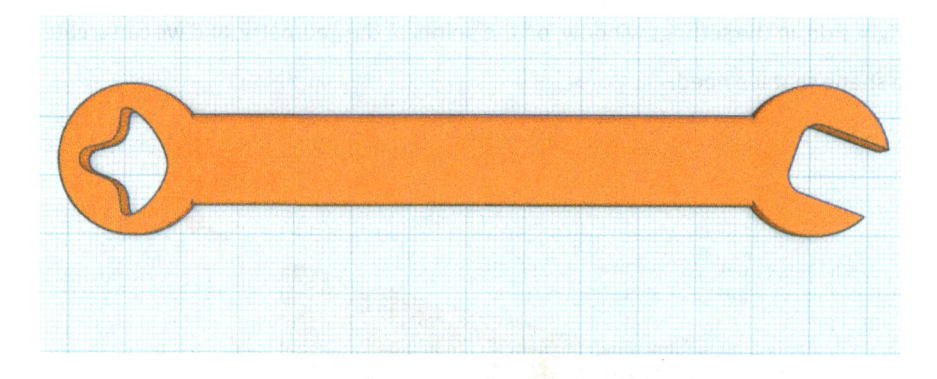

3.5 Block-based Design with Tinkercad

In addition to the design methodology in Tinkercad presented so far, which can be compared at least very roughly to the way of working in professional design programs (SolidWorks, CATIA, Inventor, ...), there is a completely different approach in Tinkercad. You can also design block-based in Tinkercad. Normally, you know this way of working from programming, where you can create a program code in a simpler way using command blocks. By the way, we will look at this in detail in one of the next chapters.

Tinkercad | Step by Step

How this works for the CAD construction of 3D objects, we will look at below, using a chair. First of all, you can try to create such a chair as shown in the way you have already learned. You are free to choose the dimensions.

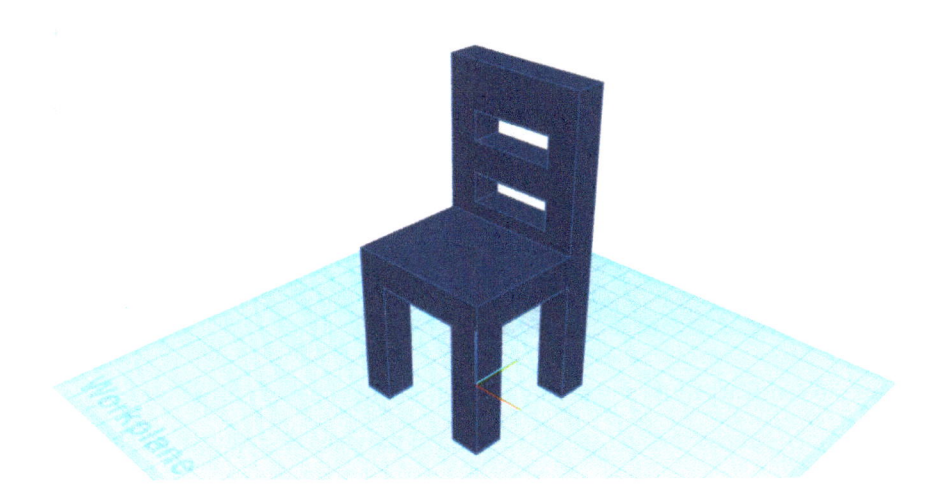

In order to design with command blocks, we need to be in the "Designs" area on the start page in Tinkercad. Here we can create a design for a block-based construction by clicking on the button "+ New" and choosing "Codeblocks".

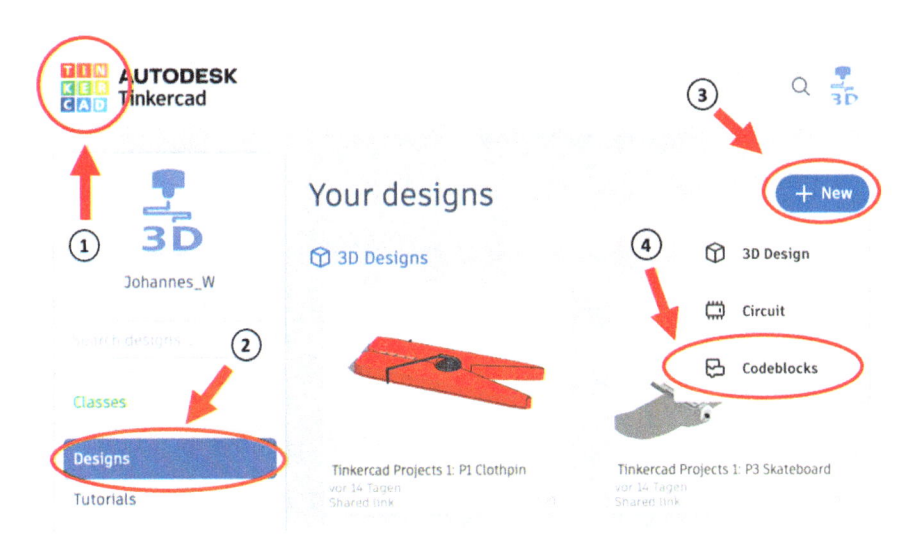

Tinkercad | Step by Step

Now we have our workspace on the left with the code blocks already specified and the 3D view we are already used to on the right. Ready to go!

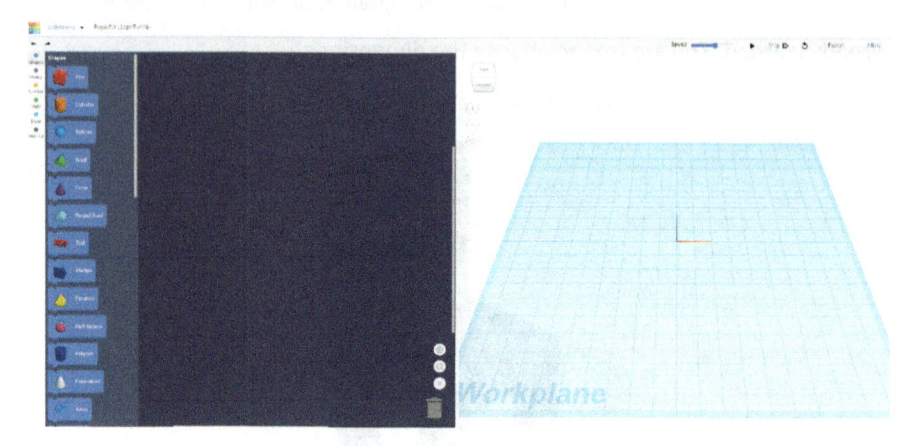

You can construct with code blocks mentally in the same way as we have done so far. What would be the first step in the case of the chair? Exactly, we would create a rectangular base body. In this case, we'll create a cube for the seat, which we'll then work on. We will add the backrest later. Now, to create this cube for the base body, we select the code block "Box" in the left pane in the "Shapes" category.

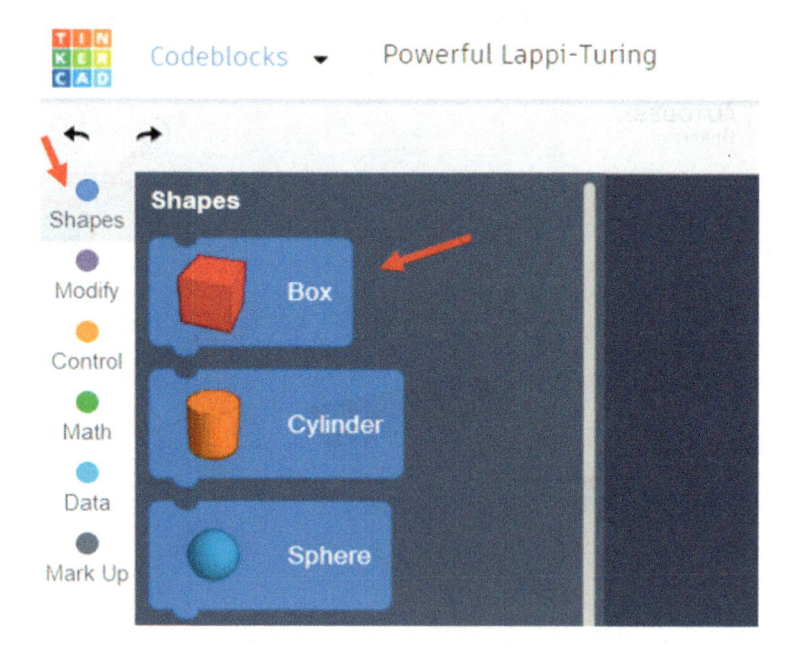

70

Tinkercad | Step by Step

We click the code block with the left mouse button, keep the mouse button pressed, and drag the block into the dark blue workspace. The appearance of the code block changes slightly to "Add" with the associated options.

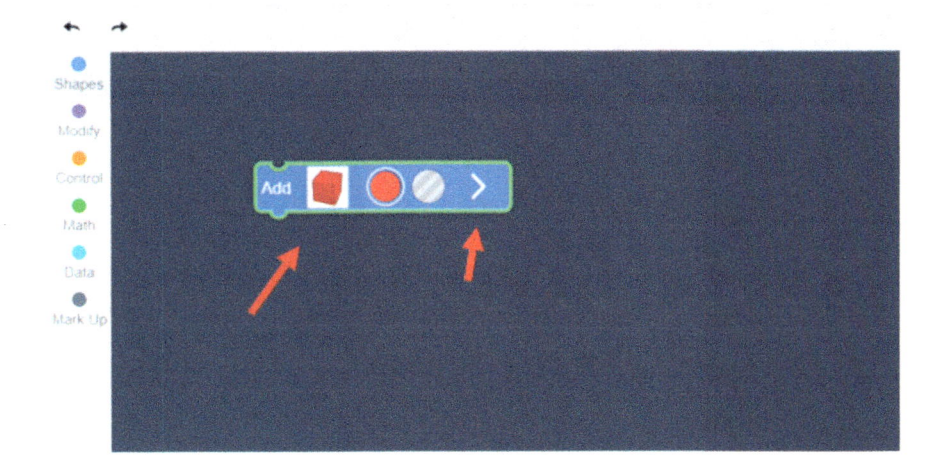

Now we have placed the first code block somewhere in the workspace. The small icon shows us which basic body we are adding to the design. To the right, we find the options "Solid" and "Hole", i.e., the settings for whether it should be a positive or negative body. By clicking on the gray arrow pointing to the right, we can open even more options, namely the options for the dimensions of the body (W x L x H = width x length x height).

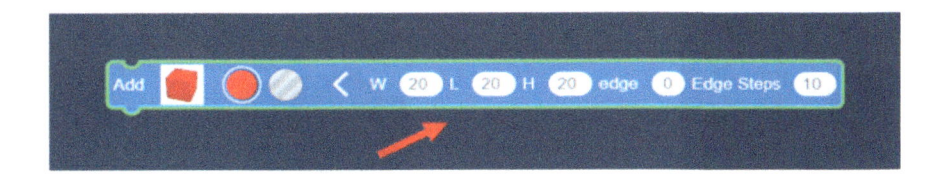

By the way, the procedure is identical for the other geometric basic bodies, e.g., cylinder or sphere.

71

Tinkercad | Step by Step

We would now like a cube with the dimensions 50 mm x 50 mm x 50 mm for the chair. Just fill in the dimensions. In addition, we still change the color to dark blue, or any other that you like.

If we now press the play icon on the right in the 3D display area in the top bar, the program will rebuild the steps that we have specified with the code blocks. Since we have only specified the creation of a blue 50x50x50 cube so far, only this will be created. Normally, the construction steps from the code blocks are animated here one after the other step by step. We will see that later.

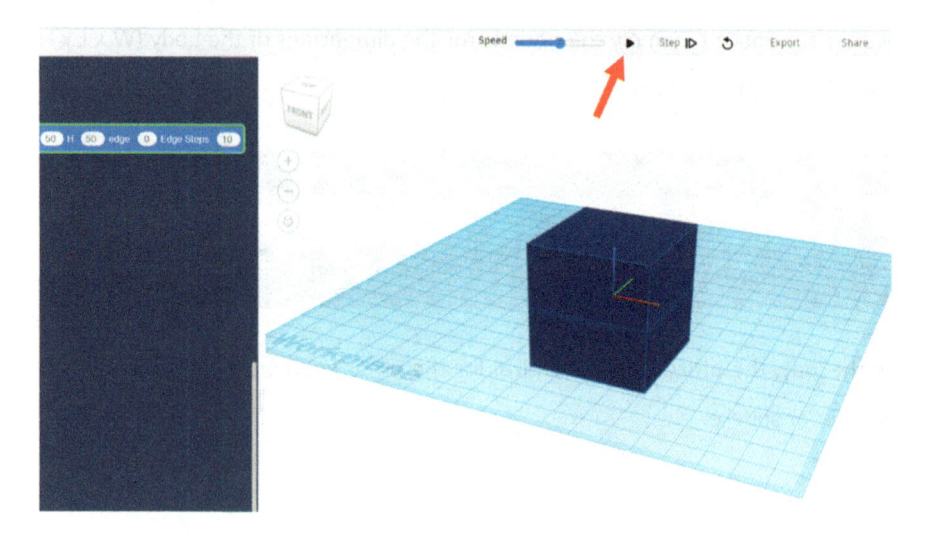

In the bar where the play icon is located, we can also adjust the speed of the animation with a slider. We can also go through each step manually with the "Step" button. With the circle arrow, we can reset the animation and start again from the beginning. The remaining two buttons, "Export" and "Share" should be self-explanatory.

By the way, if we add a body in Tinkercad this way, it will always be placed with its origin in the coordinate center of the workspace. Therefore, it protrudes above the plane both upwards and downwards. But since we only want to construct above the plane, we now have to move the cube with Move. Now you can consider the code blocks to be similar to building blocks that are simply placed on top of each other, or in this case, below each other. Like in a puzzle, the code blocks have certain shapes, so that only matching code blocks can be placed together.

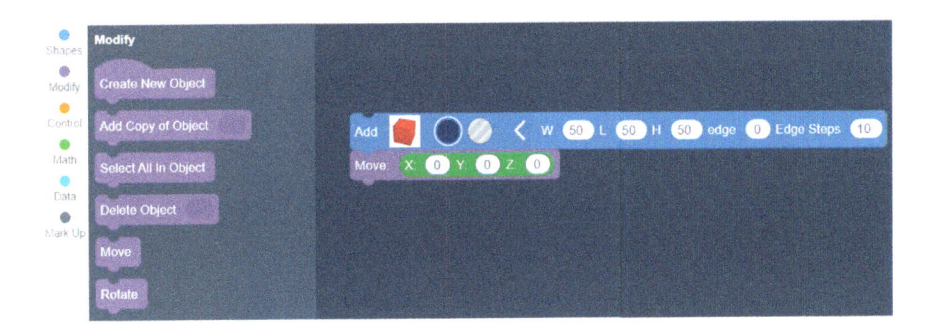

We can find the Move command in the "Modify" area. Simply select the code block on the left and drag it over to the right and dock it. You will then hear a popping sound when the block is seated correctly. With Move, we can now move the body created above it in three-dimensional space. In this case, x and y represent horizontal and vertical movement in the plane, respectively, and z represents movement out of the plane up or down. The sign in front of the value determines the direction, i.e., left, right, up or down. In our case, we need a +25 mm movement

Tinkercad | Step by Step

upwards so that the cube sits with its bottom side on the working plane. 25 mm because the coordinate system sits exactly in the center, i.e., halfway up (50 mm / 2 = 25 mm) the cube. In x-direction and in y-direction we do not have to make any displacement.

A click on the "Play" or "Step" or "Next" symbol then animates the shift. Now we have the basic body. Now we have to add the backrest. We will then make cutouts from the basic cube in the lower and inner areas, so that we get only one seat and four chair legs.

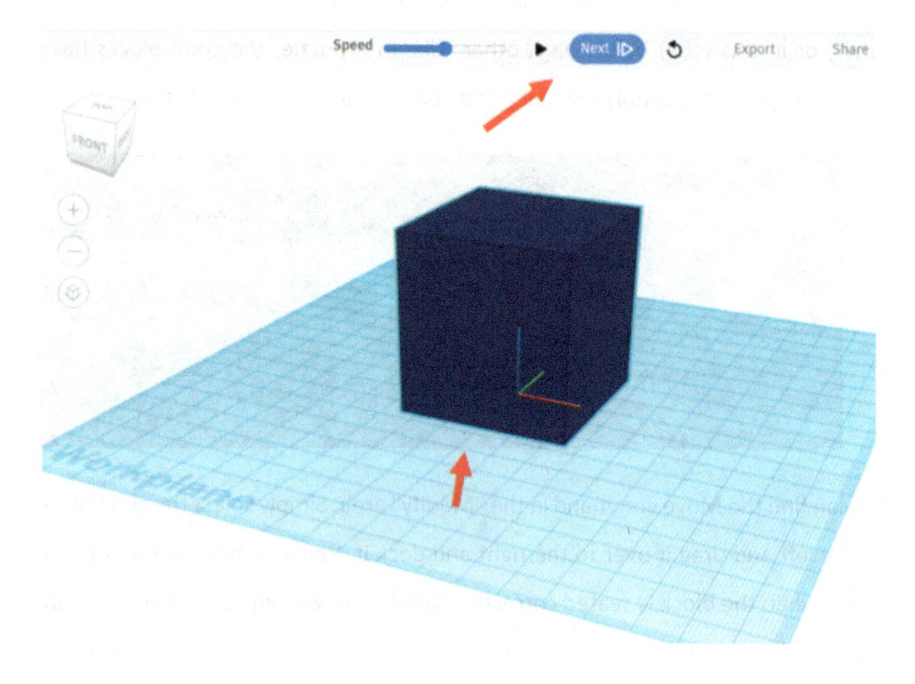

For the backrest, we again create a rectangular base body in the same color and with the dimensions: 50 x 10 x 50 mm. For this, we need another code block, which we simply add again below our blocks.

Tinkercad | Step by Step

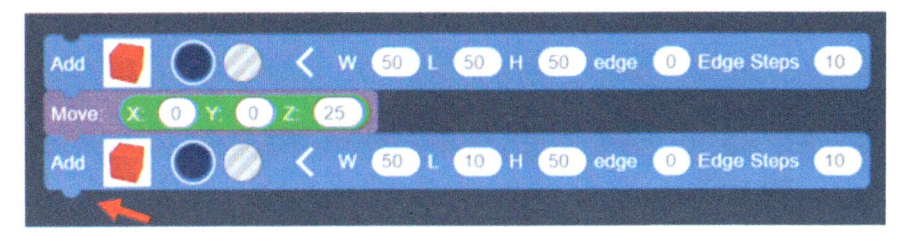

We want to move the body now also immediately, since this will appear otherwise again in the origin. I have already tried the correct coordinates for the displacement before. These are: x = 0, y = 20, z = 75.

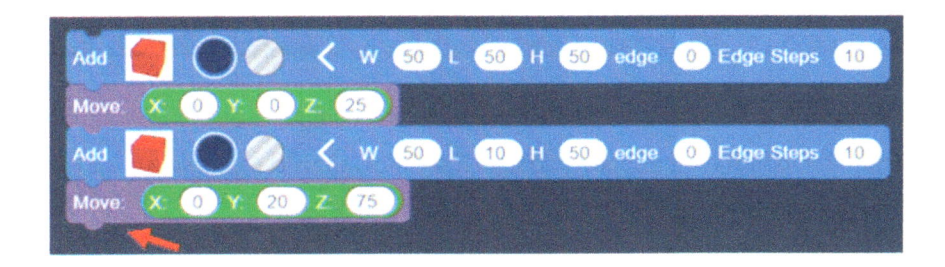

If we then let the animation continue, we get the following model:

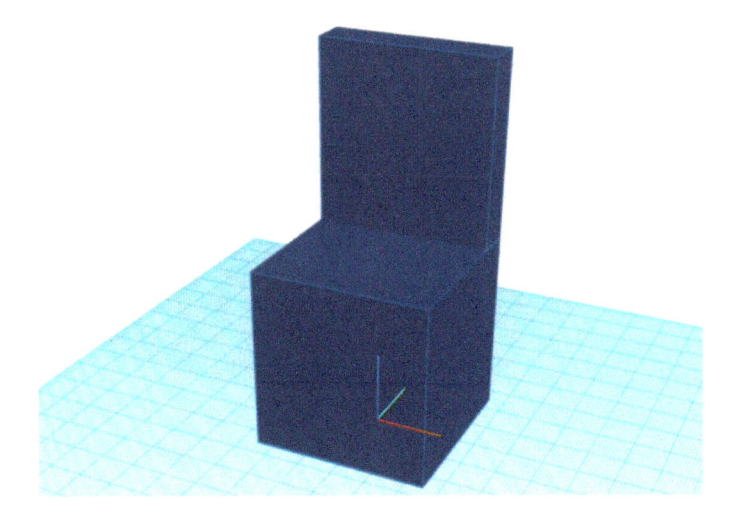

So that we now get the chair legs, we can remove the excess material in the area of the lower cube. To do this, we now create two negative solids. First we create a

75

Tinkercad | Step by Step

negative body with the dimensions 50 x 30 x 40 mm and move it with x = 0, y = 0, z = 20.

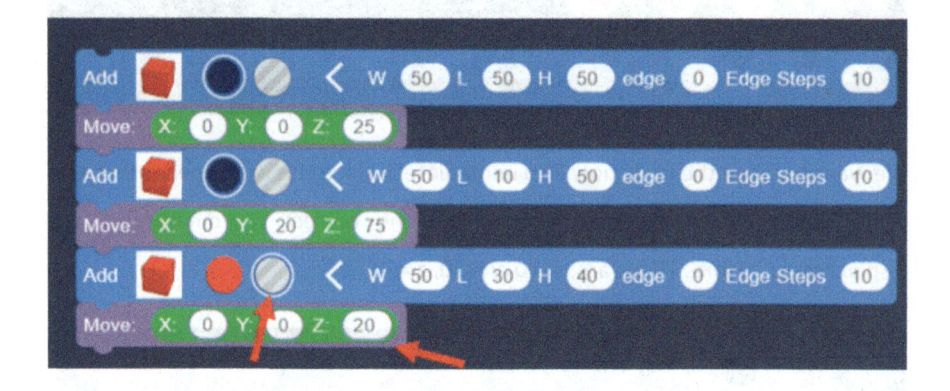

This gives us a negative body in the horizontal direction. We would now normally group this with the other body to obtain a section. In this case, however, we will do the grouping later.

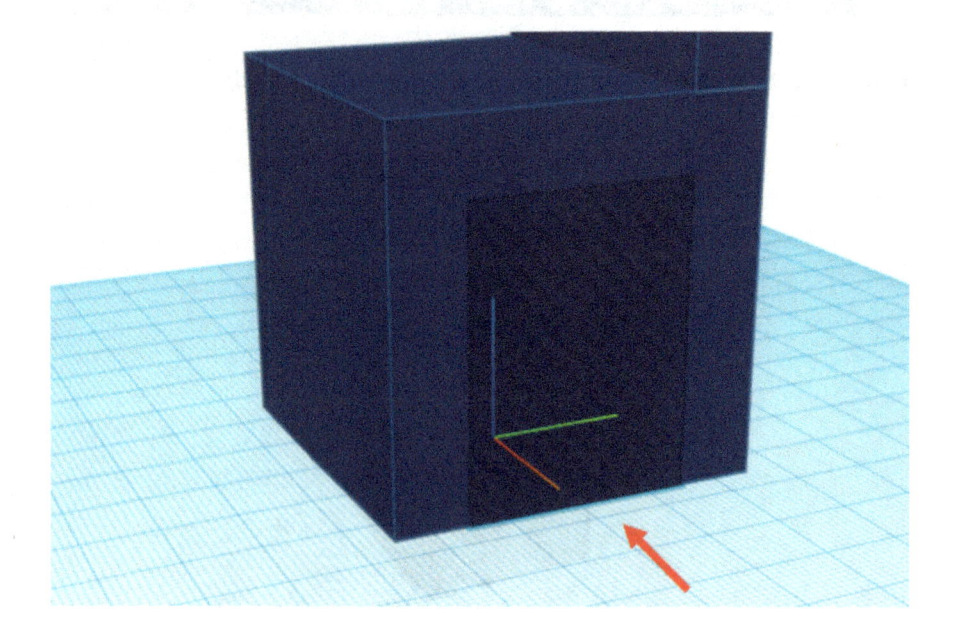

Tinkercad | Step by Step

For the other direction, we need a similar negative body. Only the dimensions are reversed here. We need 30 x 50 x 40 mm. In addition, we also move this body again by 20 mm in the z-direction.

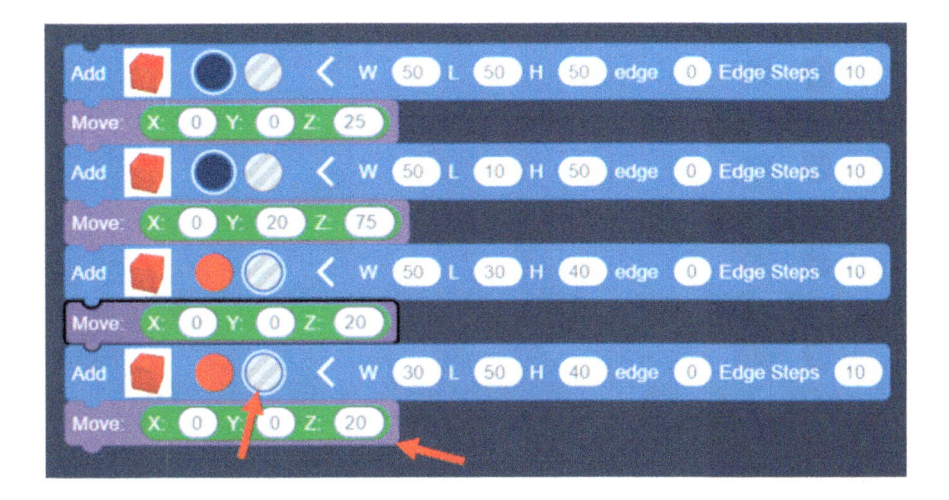

Then we add two negative bodies for the backrest and move them.

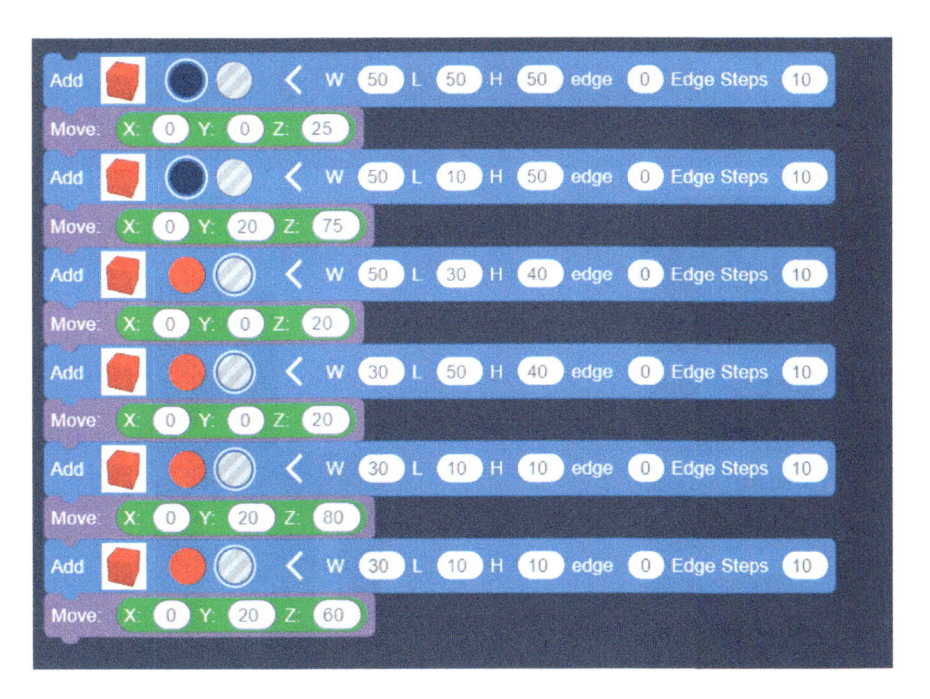

Tinkercad | Step by Step

Lastly, we use the two code blocks "Select all in Object" and "Group" so that we create a connection between each body and get the finished chair. Then just press play and watch the construction.

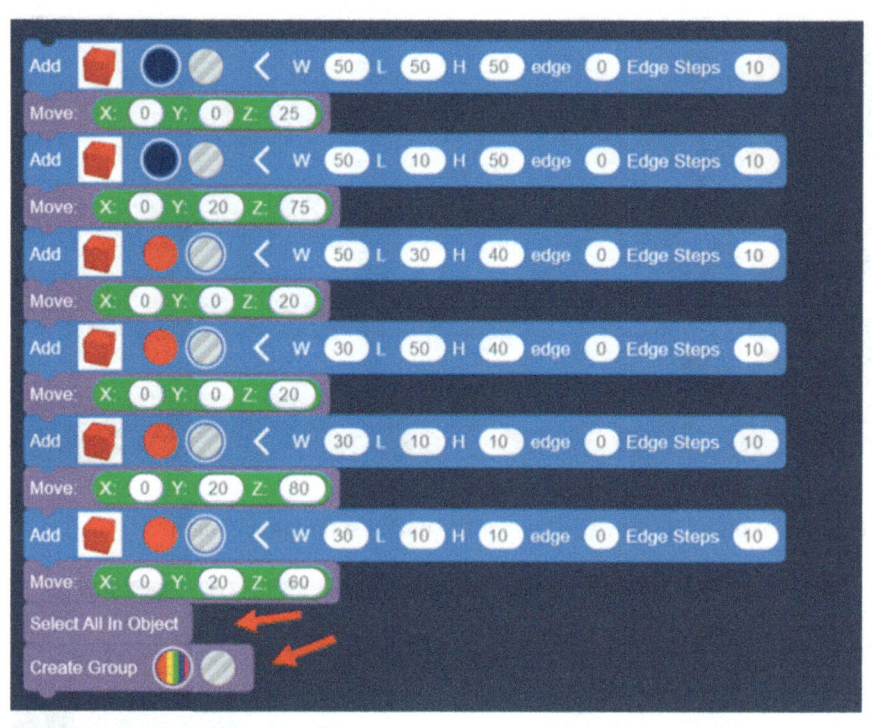

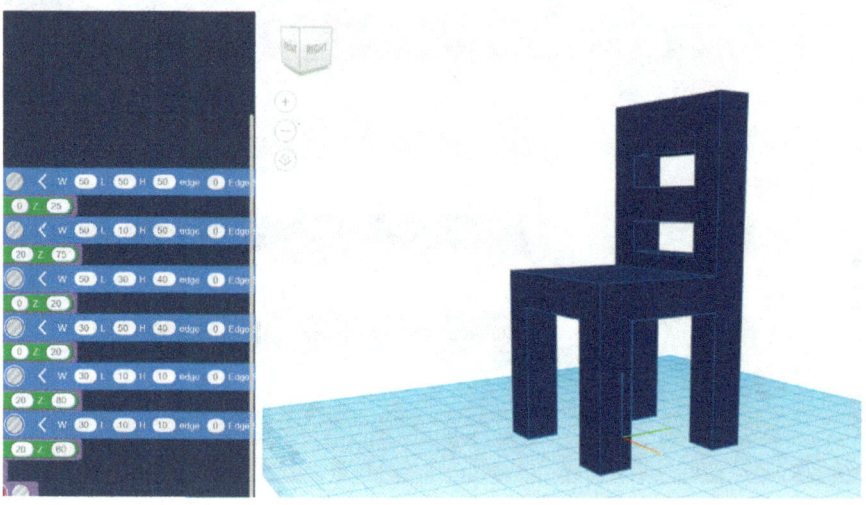

78

Tinkercad | Step by Step

4 Electronic circuits with Tinkercad

4.1 Create an electronic circuit in Tinkercad

Now we get to the second part of this course. As already mentioned, with Tinkercad you can not only design, i.e., realize mechanical projects, but also design electronic circuits and work with the mini-PC Arduino, for example. How this works, we will look at step by step and in detail in this chapter.

First a warning: *Electricity, especially alternating current and high currents, are life-threatening. If you want to build your circuits in real life and not only on the PC, then you better get someone who already knows the subject well.*

To design electronic circuits, we need to be in the "Designs" section on Tinkercad's start page. Here we can create a new circuit with selecting "+ New" and "Circuit".

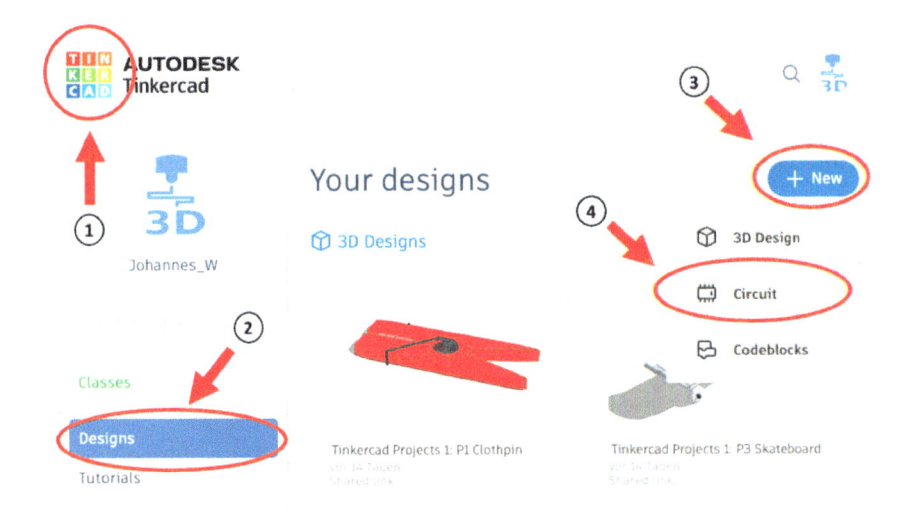

But before we do that, let's first learn some background information about current and voltage as we dive into the world of electrical engineering.

79

4.2 Background knowledge – Fundamentals of electrical engineering

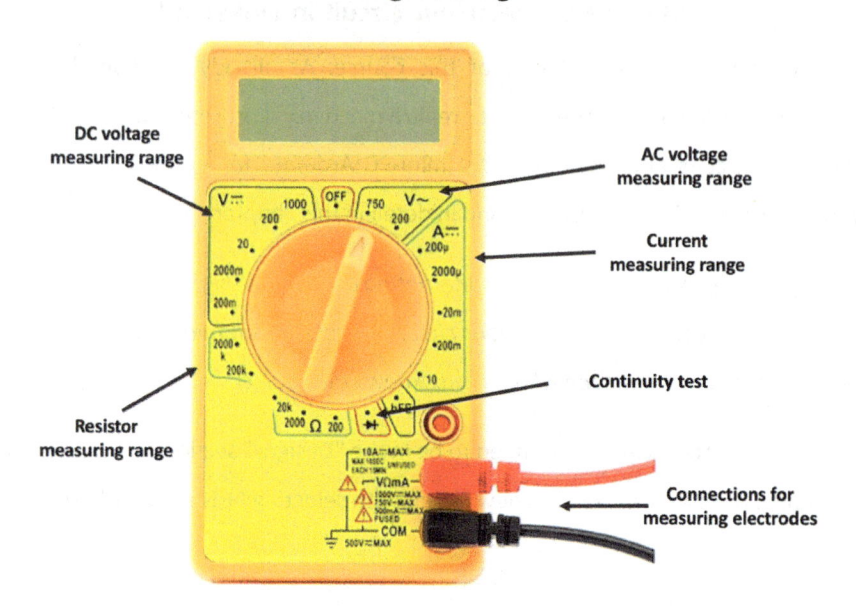

[Figure: Multimeter with labels — DC voltage measuring range, AC voltage measuring range, Current measuring range, Continuity test, Connections for measuring electrodes, Resistor measuring range]

4.2.1 Electricity

Electricity is created by electrons flowing from a place with higher potential (higher energy) to a place with lower potential (lower energy). It can be relatively well imagined by means of a waterfall. The water (represents the electrons) flows from the top point of the waterfall (high potential, high potential energy) to the bottom point of the waterfall (low potential, lower potential energy). The potential energy is transformed into kinetic energy during this process, that's why it "loses" this high-energy state in the process (but actually this energy is transformed, as said before). Similarly, the electron wants to flow from a place with higher voltage (high potential) to a place with lower voltage (low potential).

Voltage is the unit of electrical energy "generated" by the battery. The battery or any other voltage source has two terminals. One terminal is called the negative terminal and the other terminal is called the positive terminal. At the positive terminal, the voltage potential is higher than compared to the negative side. Thus, the current flows from the positive side (plus pole) to the negative side (minus pole), considering the technical direction of current.

You can think of a battery or other power-generating source as functioning like a pump. A battery, for example, "generates" voltage or energy through an electrochemical reaction inside (conversion of energy). This voltage or energy flows out of the positive pole in the form of electrons (these electrons symbolize the water molecules that are pumped out). In order to compensate for the "lost" electrons, the battery (similar to a suction pump) draws the same number of electrons back in through the negative pole.

4.2.2 Circuit

What is a circuit? Simply put, a circuit is an arrangement of different components with an electrically conductive connection between them. For an electrical circuit or circuit to work, you need an energy source / current source, such as a battery and a consumer, such as a light bulb, as well as connections between these two components, which are called conductors. In electrical engineering, these components are represented in a circuit as symbols as follows:

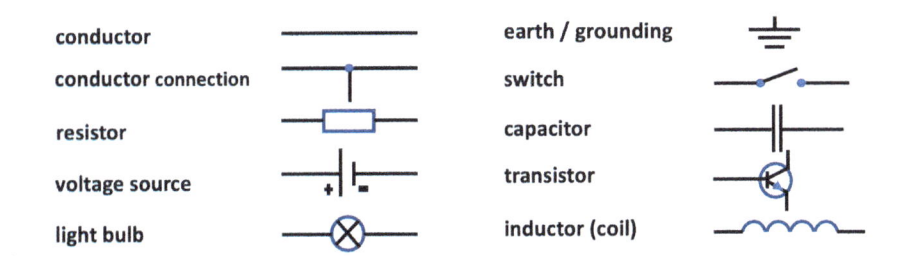

conductor	————	earth / grounding	⏚
conductor connection	─┬─	switch	─/─
resistor	─▭─	capacitor	─┤├─
voltage source	─┤├─	transistor	⊗
light bulb	─⊗─	inductor (coil)	─∿∿∿─

For a lamp, for example, to light up as shown in the following figure, the circuit must be closed, i.e., there must be a connection between the two poles (+ and -) of a power source (e.g., battery) and the incandescent lamp. If this is the case, current flows from one pole of the power source (e.g., battery) through the incandescent lamp and back to the other pole of the power source. When this connection is severed, e.g., by a switch, current no longer flows and the lamp no longer lights. In this case, it is called an open circuit. A short circuit occurs if the current can flow from one pole of the current source to the other pole unhindered and without first passing through an electrical component (e.g., through an uninsulated point of a cable on a metal surface). This is because the current always takes the path of the least resistance.

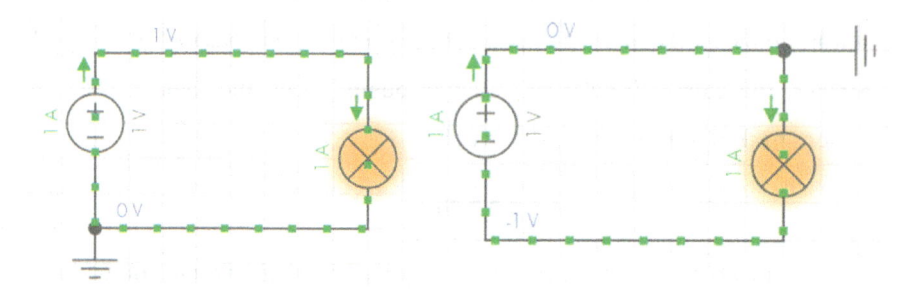

A circuit diagram is the basic concept of an electrotechnical circuit, which can be drawn, for example, on a piece of paper or with the help of a computer program (see picture above).

Such a circuit diagram can also be made a bit more descriptive (see picture below). One can create such schematics, e.g., for the mini PC Arduino, in Tinkercad. As we can see on the picture below, in this case e.g., an LED with a resistor is connected to an Arduino Uno via colored cables. The colors of the wires each have a meaning that helps to make a correct wiring. Generally, red wires are used to connect to the positive pole of a power source in DC and black wires are used to connect to the negative pole of a power source. For alternating current, there are other colors and designations, but we will not explain them here.

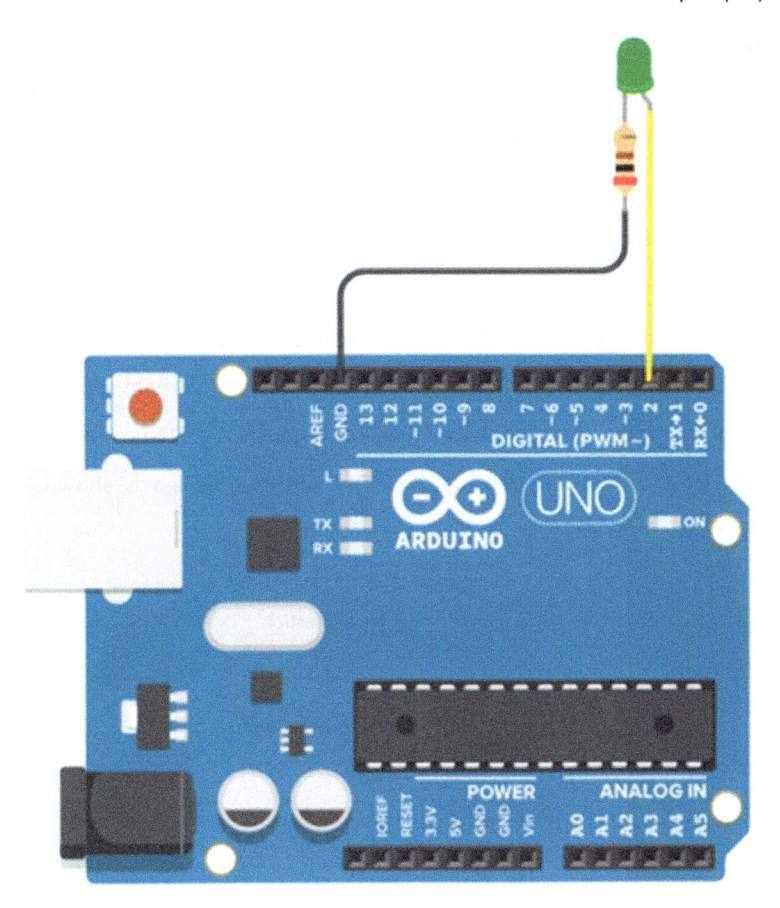

4.2.3 The diode and the light-emitting diode (LED)

A diode is a semiconductor component in electronics that has the property of allowing current to flow in only one direction (forward direction). The other direction is blocked for the current flow (reverse direction). You can imagine a diode simply like a valve.

The simplest application of a diode is the LED. The LED (light-emitting diode) is a semiconductor device that produces light when it is energized. The light is produced by current flowing from a DC source to the diode and through it. Since an LED is a semiconductor device, it also has a forward direction. This means that current can only flow through it in that direction. If an LED is connected incorrectly, no light will be produced. The color of the light and whether it is visible or not (e.g., infrared; generally determined by wavelength) is controlled by the doping and material used. Two major advantages of LEDs are: a) long life, b) low-power consumption. Compared to old-fashioned incandescent lamps, an LED can achieve a lifetime of several 10,000 hours and has many times better efficiency. Why is that? Conventional incandescent lamps produce an enormous amount of heat in addition to visible light, which means that the energy expended is converted not only into light, but primarily into heat. With LEDs, only a little heat is produced as a "waste or by-product" and almost all the energy can be used to produce the light. There are now different types of LEDs. The simplest design is shown in the following figure.

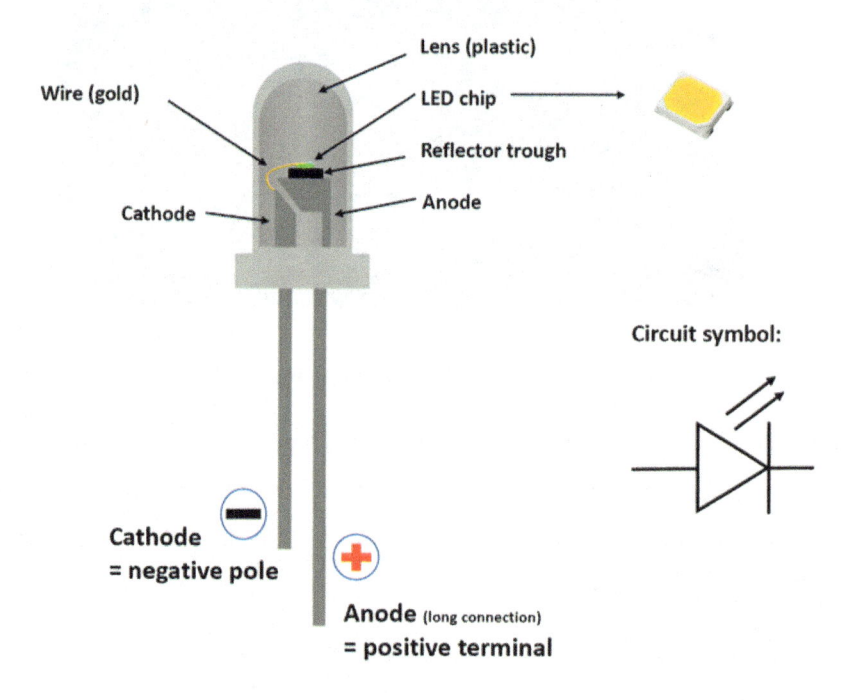

The heart and also the actual semiconductor element of the LED shown is the LED chip, which is placed on a reflector on the anode and emits the light. The circuit symbol of an LED consists of the diode circuit symbol with two additional oblique arrows, which are supposed to represent emitting light.

4.2.4 The resistance

Resistors are components that can be used primarily to apply resistance to something. In this case, the resistor acts against the flow of current and can be used to limit the flow of current into a component that is connected to the resistor. Basically, every conductor (wire or similar) has a resistance that can be calculated depending on its length and cross-section. In our case, we use so-called sheet resistors (a design form of a resistor). Here, for example, there are the carbon film resistors and the metal or also metal oxide film resistors. With these types, the resistance value comes from a ceramic core with a layer of carbon or metal or metal-oxide. The resistance value can be measured either with the help of a multimeter or directly on the resistor by means of the colored rings. Each resistor has a color code consisting of 5 rings that reveal the resistance value. How to read this color coding must be explained in detail and would therefore go beyond the scope of this chapter. One can easily look up this coding online.

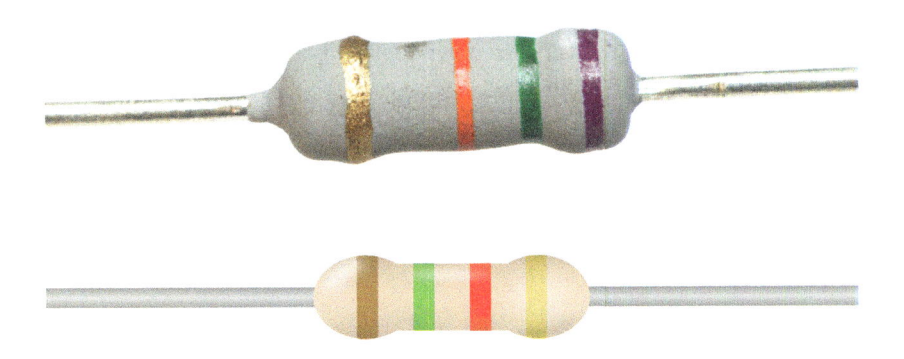

Tinkercad | Step by Step

4.3 Working environment: "Circuits"

Now let's look at how we can create circuits in Tinkercad. Once we have created a new "Circuit" project, the workspace for creating electrical engineering circuits will open.

Before we create our first circuit and then move on to a few different projects that we will create together step by step, let's first take a look at the working environment and its features.

The gray area, which in this case has no grid or anything similar, is our work plane where we design our circuits. With the help of the mouse wheel, you can also use the zoom function here. You can also move the components by holding down the left mouse button, holding down the right mouse button, or holding down the mouse wheel. With the rectangle symbol in the upper-left corner, we can fit the components into the window ("Zoom to fit"), which zooms them to an appropriate size.

Tinkercad | Step by Step

On the right side are all available electronic components, such as an LED, a resistor, a switch, a capacitor, or a battery. There is also a search function here and the possibility to display even more components (switch from "Basic" to "All" in the dropdown menu). In addition, you can switch to another arrangement, the list view, with the small list icon in the upper-right corner. Just try it out. In the list view, you also get a short description of each component.

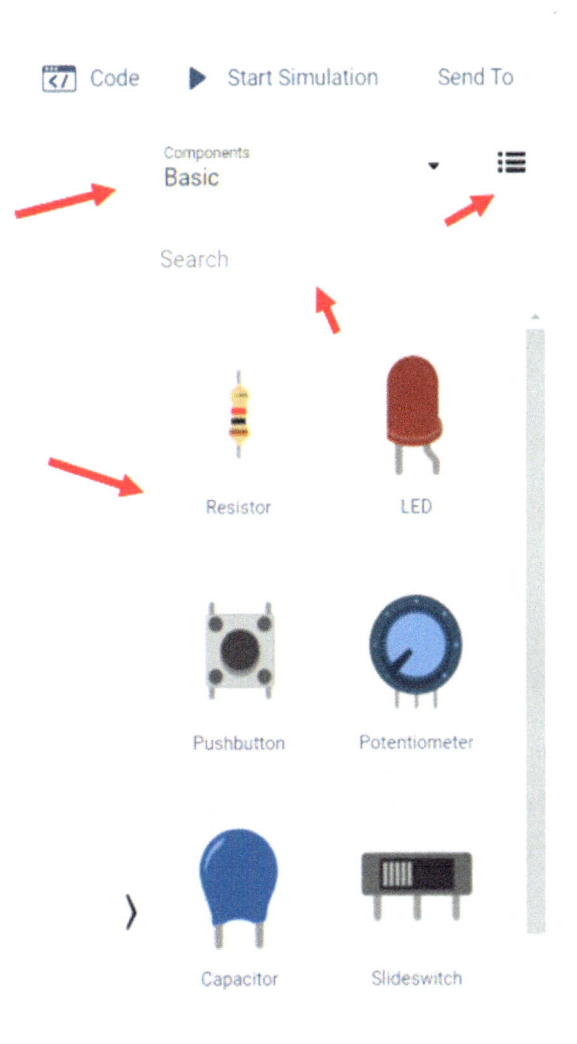

To add a component to your circuit, you just have to click on it and then move to the working area (left) with the computer mouse. With another click, you can place

87

Tinkercad | Step by Step

the component at any position. Let's do this for example with a resistor. As soon as we have placed it, a small window opens in the upper-right corner where we can make settings for the component. Here we can assign a name and in the case of the resistor, set the resistance, e.g., 1 kOhm (1000 Ohm). We can open this settings window by clicking on the component and close it again by clicking in the layer.

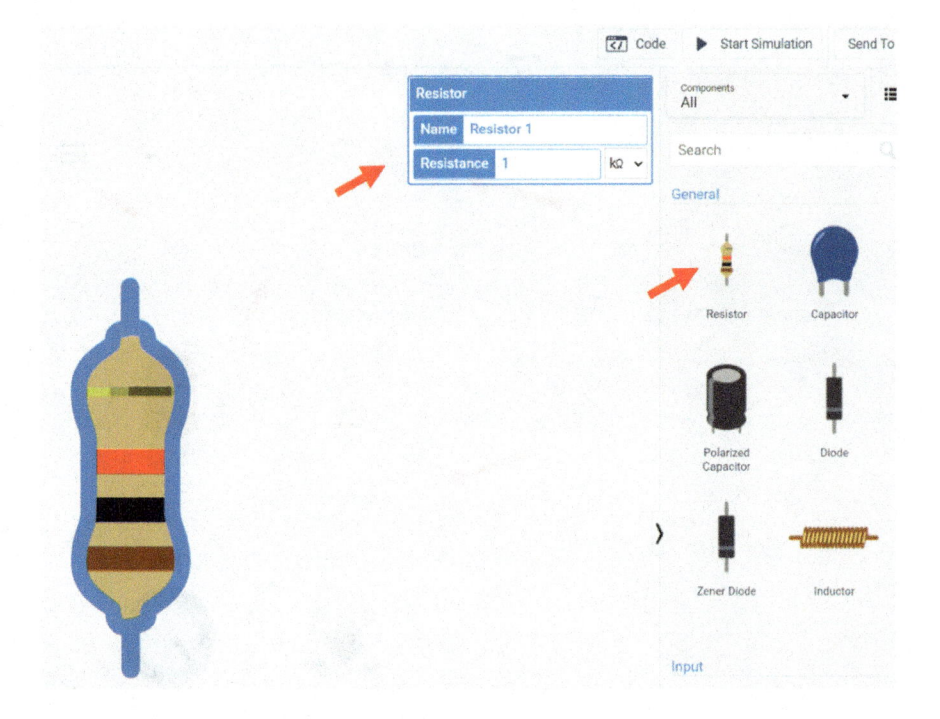

In the upper-left area we find another bar, with which we can again perform basic functions, such as rotate, delete, undo and redo. In addition, here we can control the note tool and the visibility of notes and change the color and type of wires.

88

Tinkercad | Step by Step

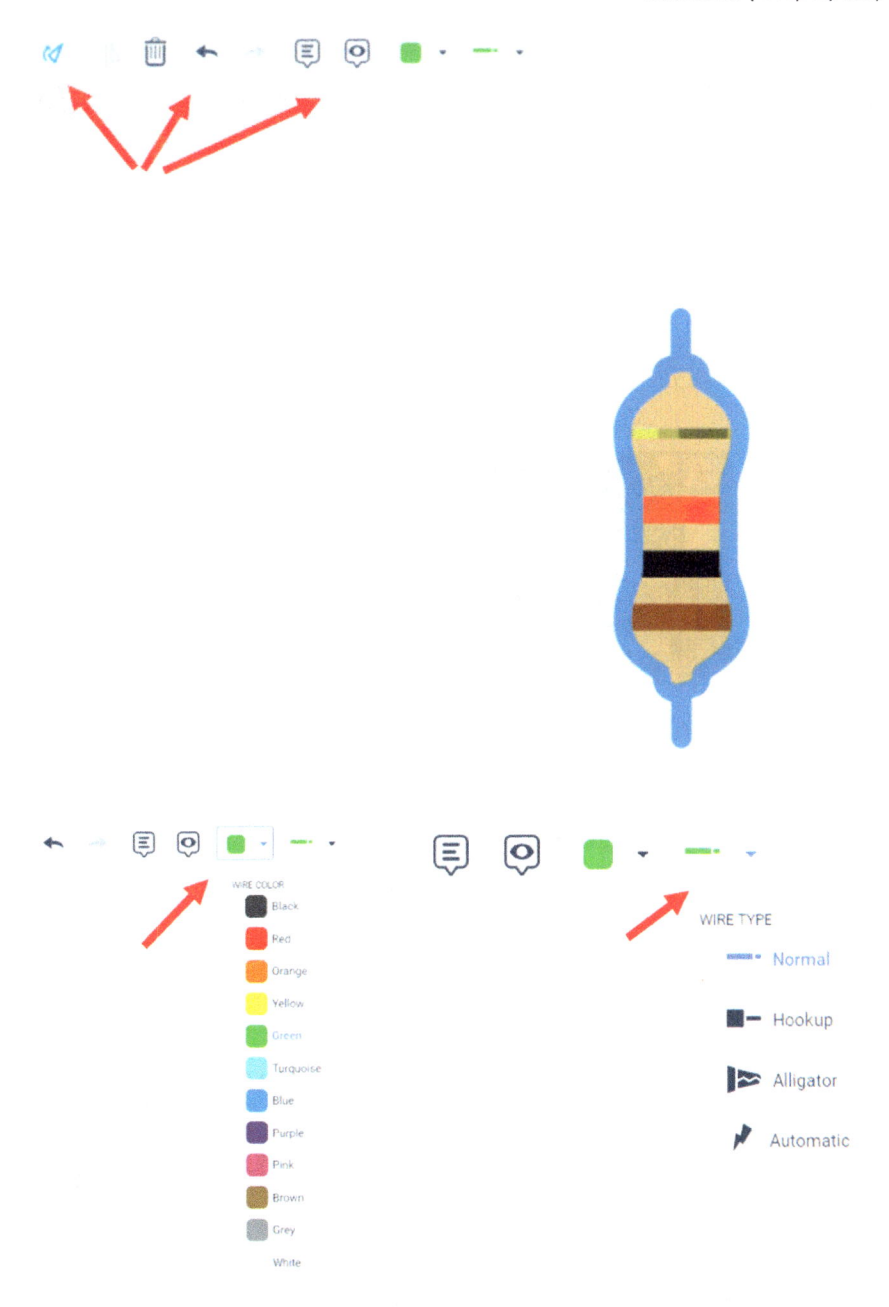

WIRE COLOR
- Black
- Red
- Orange
- Yellow
- Green
- Turquoise
- Blue
- Purple
- Pink
- Brown
- Grey
- White

WIRE TYPE
- Normal
- Hookup
- Alligator
- Automatic

89

Tinkercad | Step by Step

If you have a programmable component such as an Arduino Mini-PC in your circuit, you can use the "Code" button in the top right-hand area to create or display a program code. We will have a closer look at this area in the next chapter.

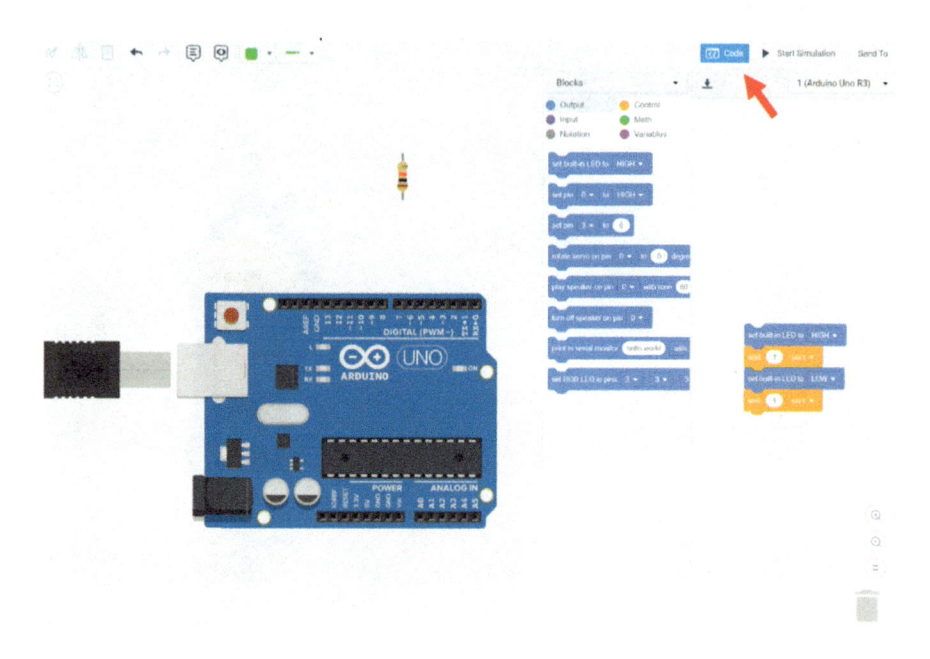

With the button "Start Simulation" the created circuit can even be simulated, so you can test here in a safe virtual environment whether the functioning of the circuit runs as desired.

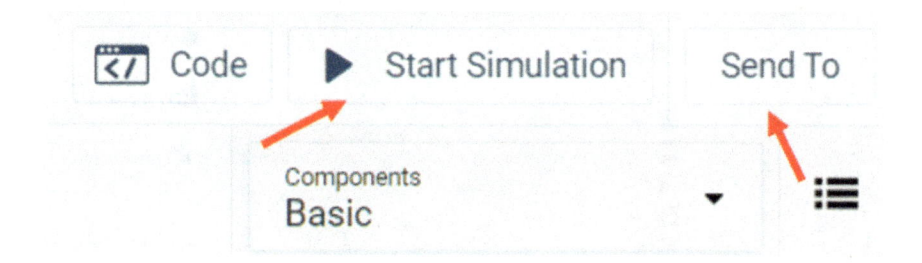

With "Send To" you can send your circuit, similar to the working environment "3D Design", or edit it further with Fusion 360 or download it as ". brd" file format.

Tinkercad | Step by Step

In the top-right area there are two very useful functions. Firstly, by clicking on the "Schematic View" area, you can convert the pictorial circuit diagram into a real schematic circuit diagram, and secondly, by clicking on "Component List", you can generate a parts list.

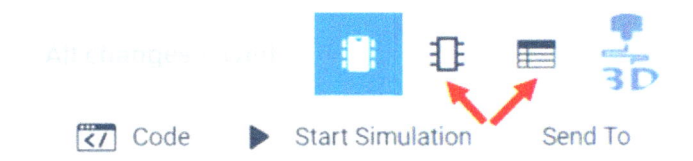

This is really very helpful! On the top right, you can save the schematic or the parts list as ". pdf" or ". csv".

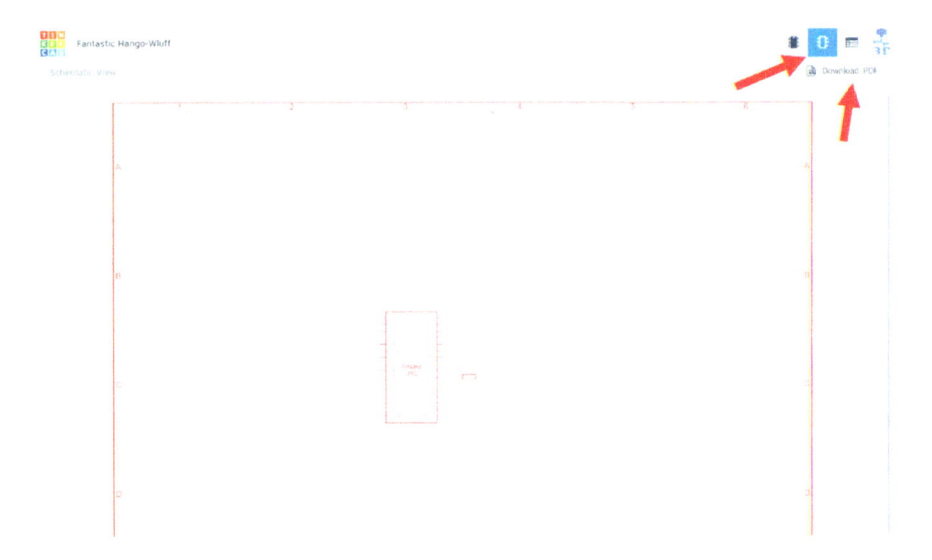

91

Tinkercad | Step by Step

Great! Now we know our way around the working environment and can start with the first circuit diagram. First, we get a so-called "breadboard" or a plug-in board into our working environment. We find this in the category "Basic", if we scroll down a bit. Just click on it and then click into the working environment to place it.

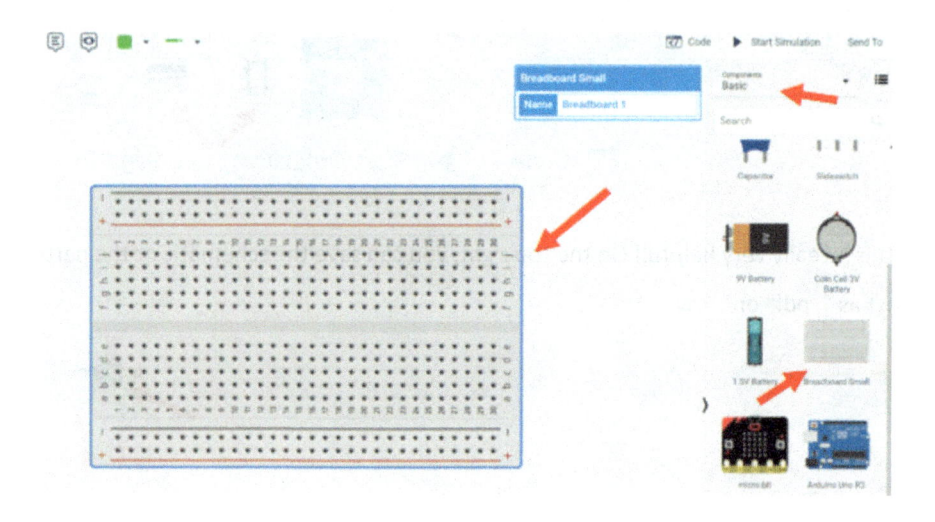

A breadboard is the best way to build a circuit as soon as it becomes a bit more complex or contains several parts. With a breadboard, there is an area for the power supply of the breadboard ("+" and "-" imprint) and areas with letters and numbers. The pins that are in a row (letters: a-e and f-j) are conductively connected to each other. That means e.g., h1 and i1 or h5 and i5 and j5 are conductively connected. The components and cables are plugged into the respective pins and thus connected to each other.

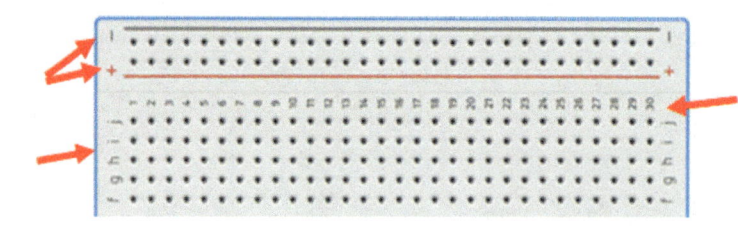

Tinkercad | Step by Step

For our first circuit, we will make an LED glow. For this, we need an LED, a resistor (1 kOhm) and a 9V battery. We will get these components into our working environment.

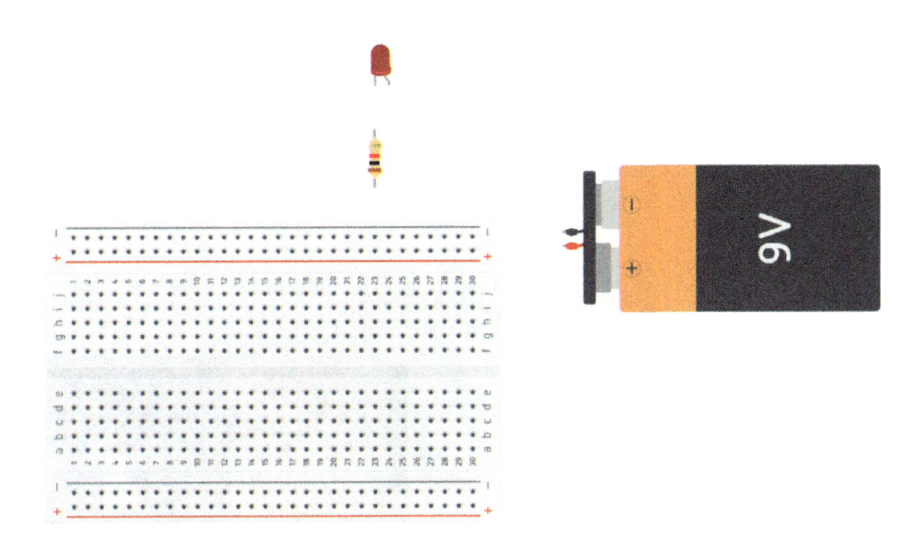

Then we need to connect the components with wires. However, we won't find any wire or line in the selection area on the right side. To create a wire, we simply click with our mouse on a pole, for example on the "+" pole of the battery. This allows us to draw a line that represents our wire.

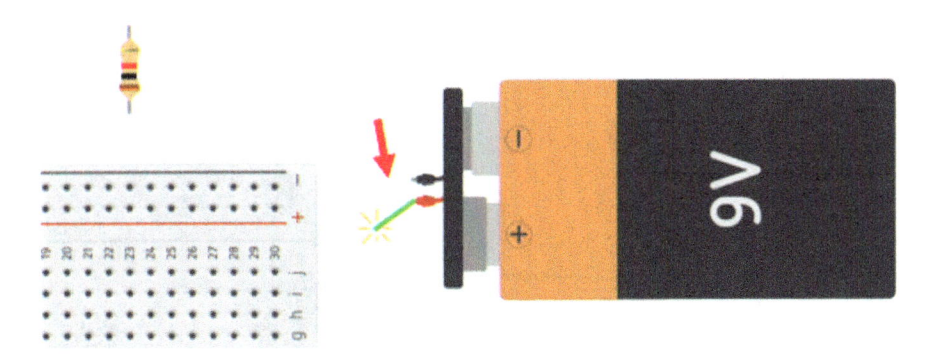

93

As the second connection point for this line, we select a slot of the "+" row of the breadboard ("+" to "+").

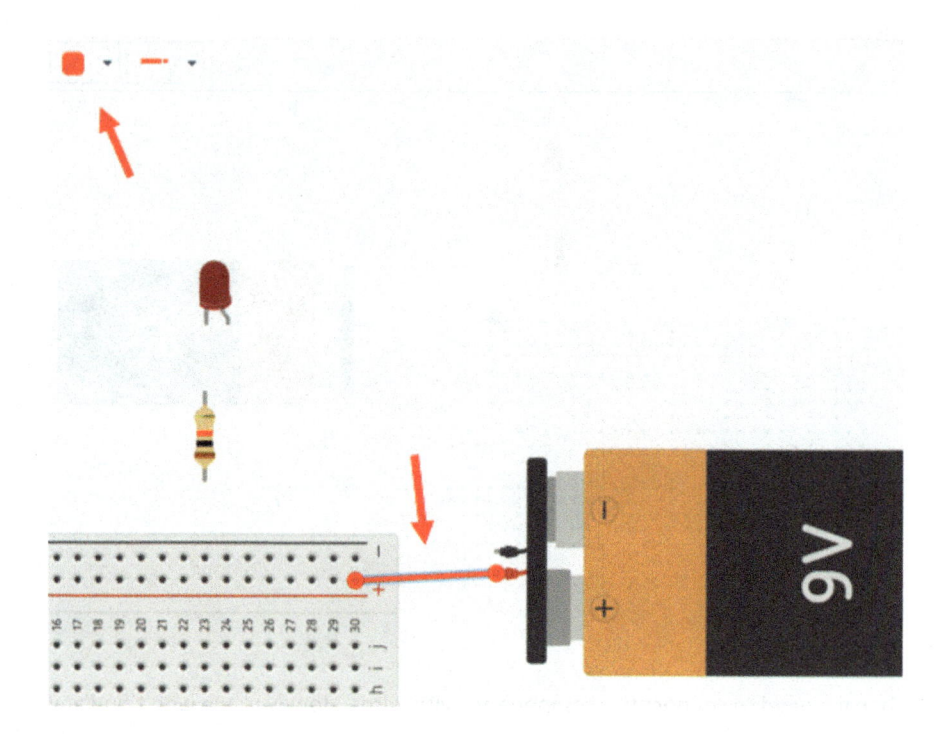

In addition, we can also give the connecting wire a different color at the same time, e.g., red (for "+"). We do the same with the negative pole of the battery. We connect it with the negative pole of the breadboard,, and we choose the color black for this "-" line. Now our breadboard has current.

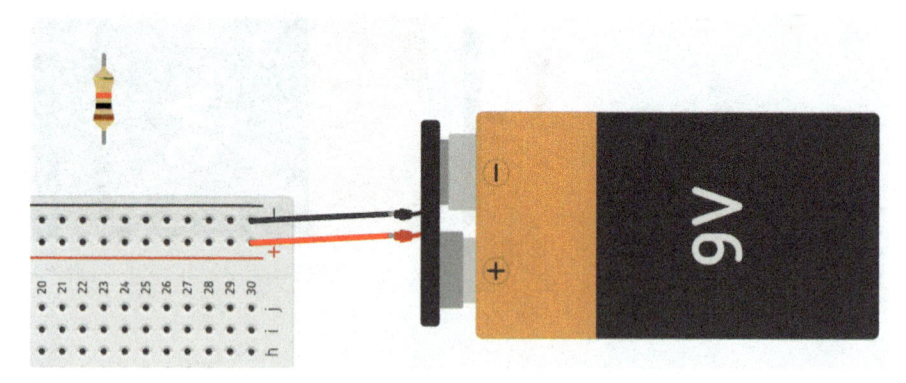

Tinkercad | Step by Step

If we click on the LED, we can determine the color of the LED in the next step. For example, we do not want to have a red LED, but a green one, in our circuit.

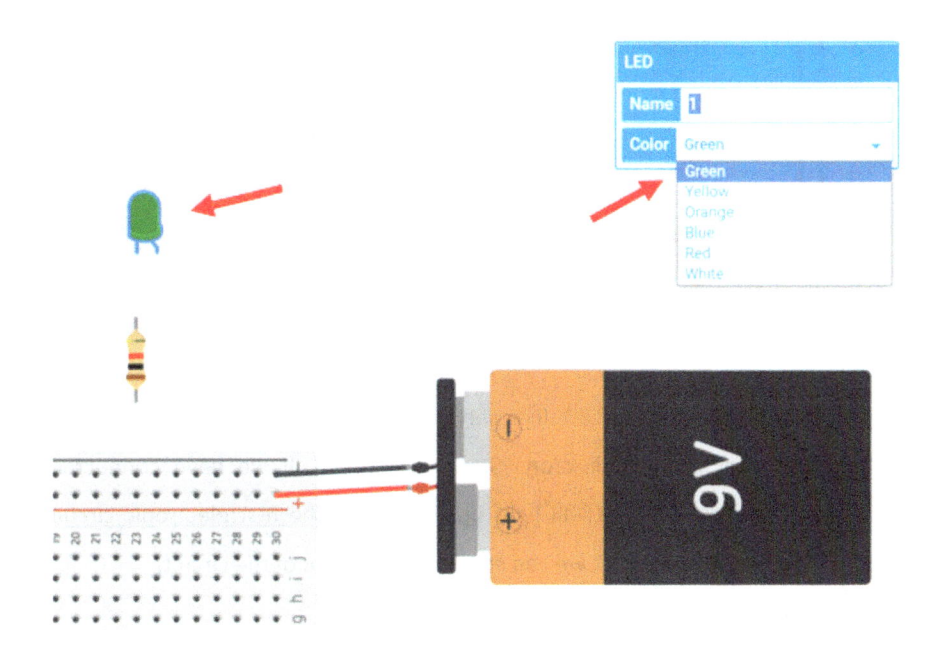

Now we can connect the resistor and the LED. The straight leg of the LED (here on the left) represents the cathode, i.e., the negative pole of the LED. We connect this to one side of the resistor – which side of the resistor doesn't matter. From the resistor, we connect another wire to the line with the negative pole of the breadboard – which slot again doesn't matter. From the positive pole of the LED, the so-called anode, we connect another line to the line with the positive pole of the breadboard – again, which slot doesn't matter. If we swap the two poles, the LED will not light up later because the LED is a diode, which lets the current through only in one direction. So, the correct connection is essential here. It is also best to choose the correct colors for the "-" (black) and "+" (red) wires for a better understanding of the circuit.

Tinkercad | Step by Step

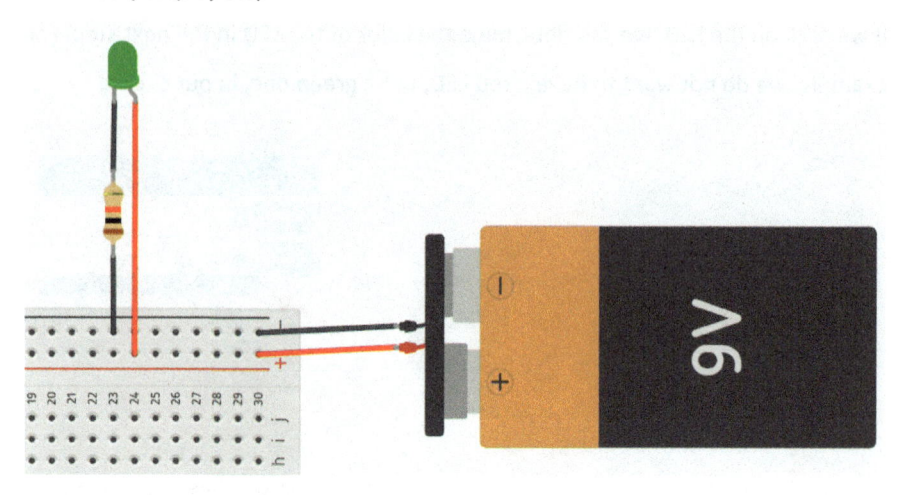

Now we have connected the LED. In reality, this would now light up immediately. In Tinkercad, we have to click on "Start Simulation". If we have connected everything correctly, the LED will light up. Fantastic! The first electronic circuit works. With "Stop Simulation" we can stop the simulation of the circuit.

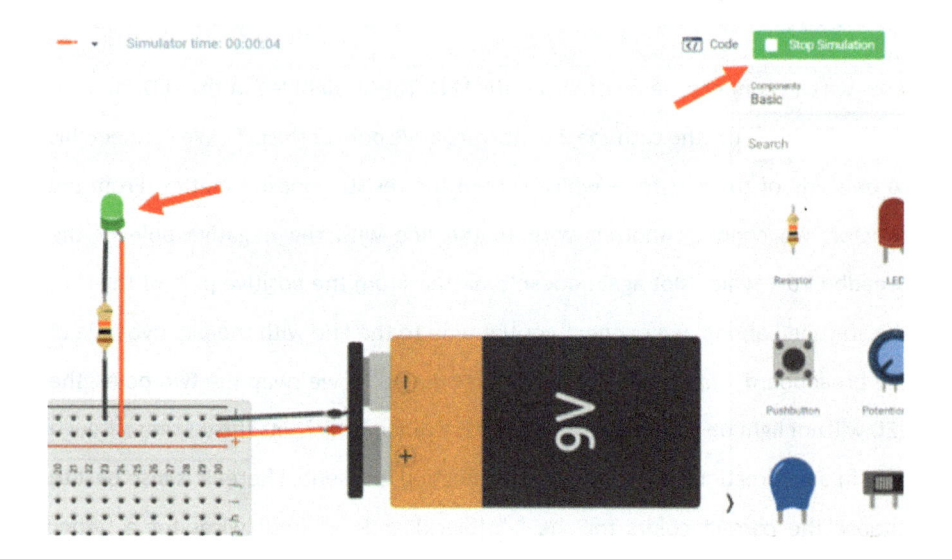

At this point, you can also swap the poles in Tinkercad and check if the LED is still on when you start the simulation.

Tinkercad | Step by Step

Now you may have wondered why we need a resistor here and not just connect the LED to the battery. We required the resistor to limit the current that flows through the LED. The current coming from the battery would be too strong for such an LED. Without a resistor, the LED would either burn out, i.e., break, or have a shortened life span. By the way, the lower the resistor, the brighter the LED shines. We can now try this out in Tinkercad by lowering the resistor value from 1 kOhm to 100 ohms and see what happens.

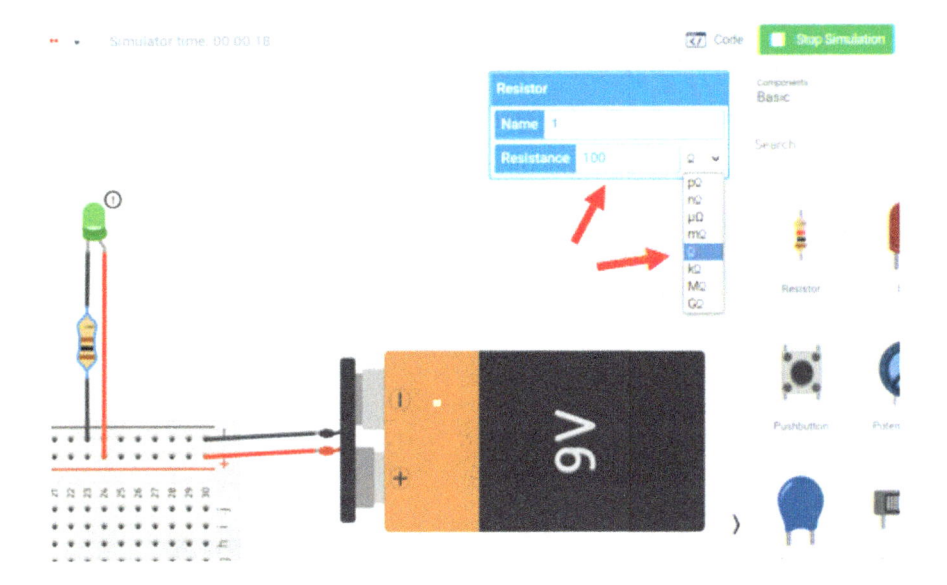

If the simulation is still running, the brightness of the LED will change, and we will see a small exclamation mark. If we move over it with the mouse, we will also see a hint text about it.

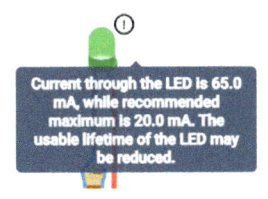

This states that the current flows through the LED at 65 mA and this is likely to reduce the lifetime of the LED. A maximum current of 20 mA is recommended.

97

4.4 "Circuit" project 1: photoresistor controls motor speed

In this first project on electrical engineering circuits, we will control a motor through a photoresistor. A photoresistor has the function of a normal resistor, i.e., it limits the current flow. The special feature of a photoresistor is that this limitation depends on the light incident on the sensor. This means that the more light falls on the sensor (e.g., because it is bright in the morning), the lower the resistance of the photoresistor becomes, and therefore the more current can flow through it. We would also like to include a manual switch in our circuit, an LED to monitor activity, and a motor. The LED and the motor should depend on the light through the photoresistor. The brighter the incident light, the brighter the LED will shine and the faster the motor will turn.

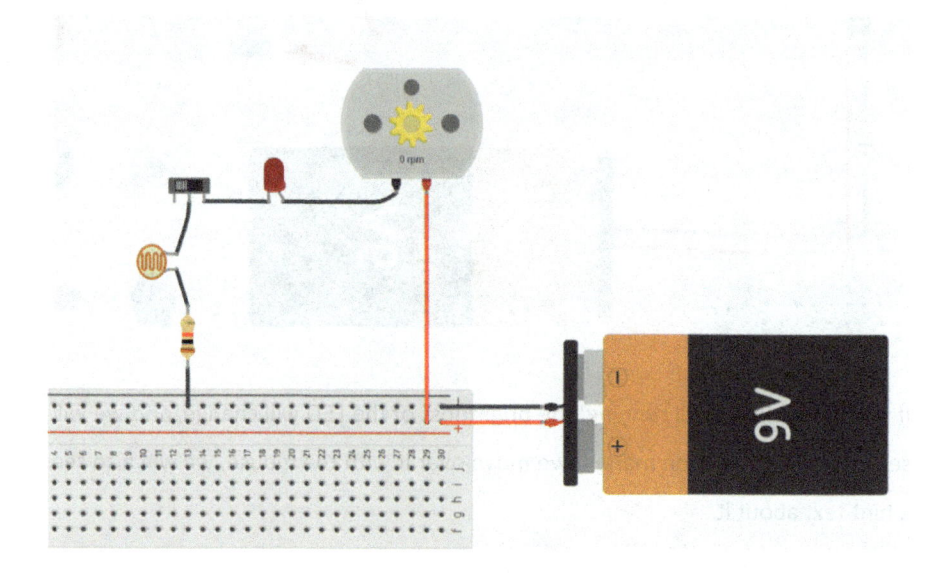

We connect all components as shown (resistance: 1kOhm).

If we now turn on the switch by clicking on it, the LED will glow dimmed and the motor will turn very slowly (of course we have to start the simulation again for this).

Tinkercad | Step by Step

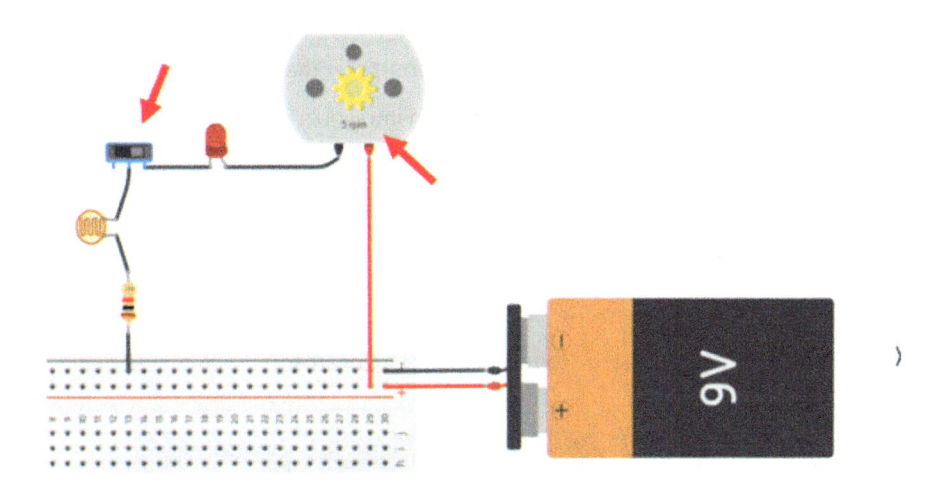

Now, if we click on the photoresistor, we can control the incident light with a slider. The higher the incident light becomes, the brighter the LED will now shine and the faster the motor will turn.

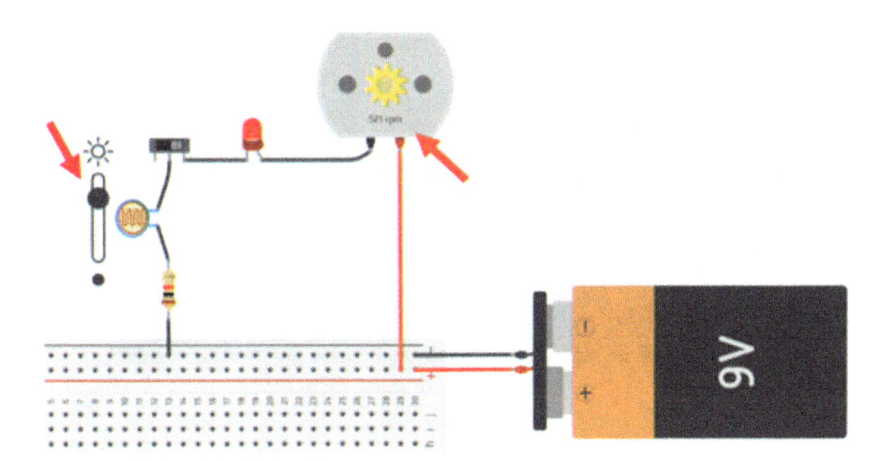

99

4.5 "Circuit" project 2: Control RGB LED with an Arduino

In this project, we will control a RGB LED with an Arduino Mini-PC, depending on the ambient temperature. What is an Arduino? Simply put, an Arduino is nothing more than a small and very simple PC or microcontroller that can take input signals, process them internally and then convert them into corresponding output signals. An input signal could be e.g., the temperature measured by a sensor. The corresponding output signal could, for example, control an LED. An Arduino can be purchased in the simple form of a circuit board, equipped with electronic components, individually or as a set. For beginners, the Arduino Uno is recommended. This can also be found virtually in Tinkercad.

If the temperature is high (e.g., higher than 25 °C), the LED should light up red in our project. On the other hand, if the temperature is low (e.g., lower than 15 °C), the LED should light up blue. When the temperature is optimal (e.g., between 15 °C and 25 °C), the LED should light up green.

Tinkercad | Step by Step

But how is this supposed to work with only one LED? We need a special LED for this, namely an RGB LED. An RGB LED can shine in three colors, namely red (r), green (g) and blue (b). The LED has two more terminals than a normal LED, and the color of the light depends on which terminal you apply power to. To control the RGB LED, connect it e.g., to PINs 3, 5, 6 of the Arduino.

To make the control dependent on the temperature, we also need a temperature sensor, e.g., the TMP36 sensor. The TMP36 provides an analog output voltage that is dependent on the temperature in degrees Celsius. The temperature range is from -40 °C to +125 °C.

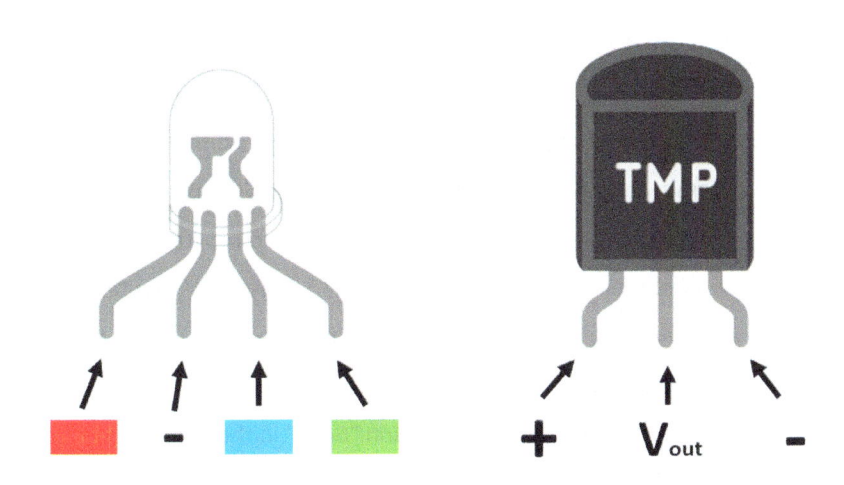

First we place the RGB LED on the breadboard and connect the connectors for the LED colors to the pins 3, 5, 6 of the Arduino and the cathode ("-") with a 200 Ohm resistor as shown below. Then we equip the breadboard with the temperature sensor and connect it as shown. The middle pin should be connected to the Arduino A0 input. Finally, we connect the 5V pin ("+") and the GND pin ("-") of the Arduino to the breadboard to provide the power supply.

101

Tinkercad | Step by Step

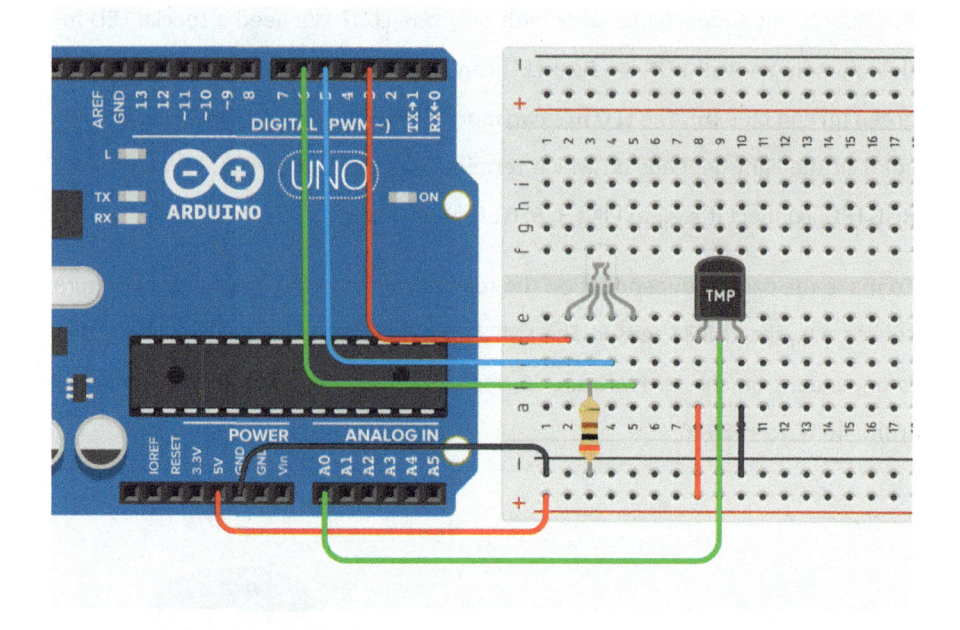

In order for our circuit to work now, we still have to instruct the Arduino with the help of a program code which signals the Arduino should pass on to the LED at which temperature. For this, we have to write a code in programming language. We will look at the procedure for this in detail in the next chapter, using an uncomplicated method in Tinkercad. For completeness of this chapter, the program code is listed below. You can simply copy or paste it. Where this code has to go, I will show you first. Click on the button "Code" in the upper-right corner of the toolbar in Tinkercad and select the option "Text" in the dropdown menu one line below. Then copy the code into the text field or write it there. Make sure that you copy the text exactly, character by character. If a character is missing, you may get an error. If this is too much work for you, then take a look at the next chapter, in which we will create the program code in an easy way.

Tinkercad | Step by Step

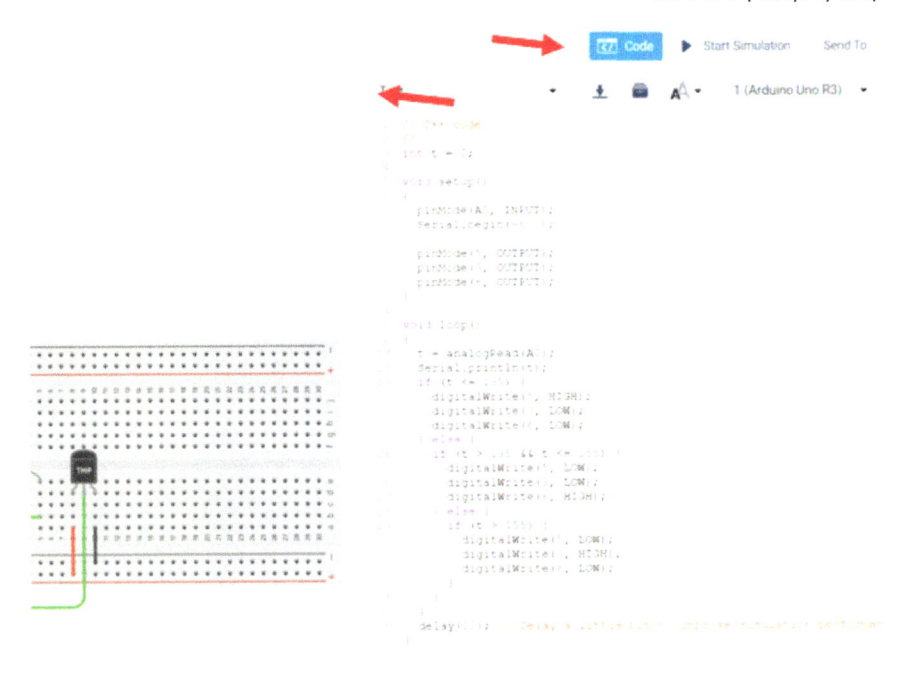

Here is the program code to copy or transcribe:

// C++ code

//

int t = 0;

void setup()
{
  pinMode(A0, INPUT);

  Serial.begin(9600);

  pinMode(5, OUTPUT);

  pinMode(3, OUTPUT);

  pinMode(6, OUTPUT);

103

}

```
void loop()
{
  t = analogRead(A0);
  Serial.println(t);
  if (t <= 135) {
    digitalWrite(5, HIGH);
    digitalWrite(3, LOW);
    digitalWrite(6, LOW);
  } else {
    if (t > 135 && t <= 155) {
      digitalWrite(5, LOW);
      digitalWrite(3, LOW);
      digitalWrite(6, HIGH);
    } else {
      if (t > 155) {
        digitalWrite(5, LOW);
        digitalWrite(3, HIGH);
        digitalWrite(6, LOW);
      }
    }
  }
  delay(10); // Delay a little bit to improve simulation performance
}
```

Tinkercad | Step by Step

Once we have entered the program code, we can start the simulation of our circuit by clicking on "Start Simulation" as usual. With a click on the temperature sensor, we can set the ambient temperature. As we can see, 25 °C is currently set, therefore the RGB LED also lights up in green as desired.

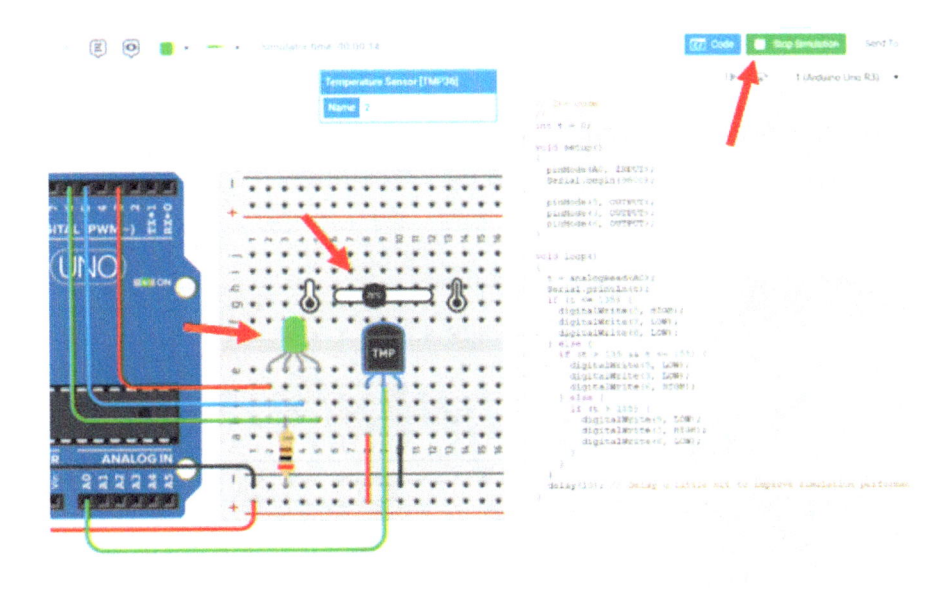

If we now set the slider of the temperature sensor below 15 °C, we will see that the RGB LED changes to a blue color.

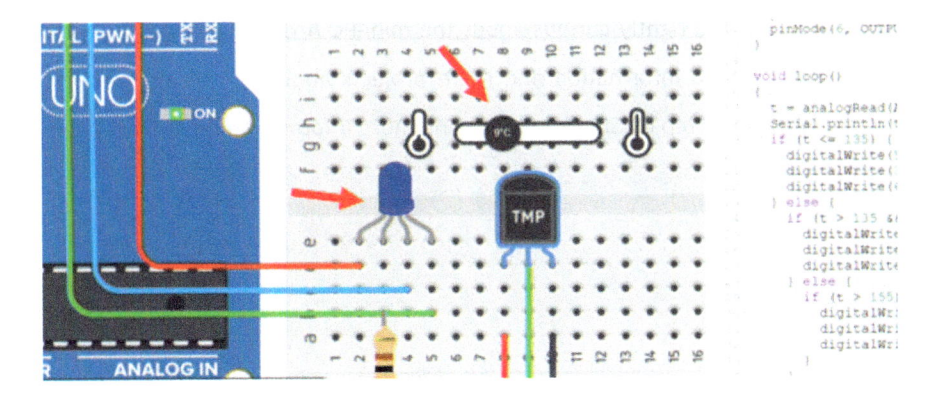

105

And if we set a temperature above 25 °C, the RGB LED should light up red. This also works flawlessly! Great!

Now we have successfully completed this project as well. In the next chapter, we will also deal with programming in Tinkercad. In this chapter, I had already given the program code, in the next chapter we want to look at how we can create it ourselves in Tinkercad in a simple way. Let's go, soon we will have learned all functions of Tinkercad. You can be proud of yourself if you already made it to this point and stuck with it. Congratulations!

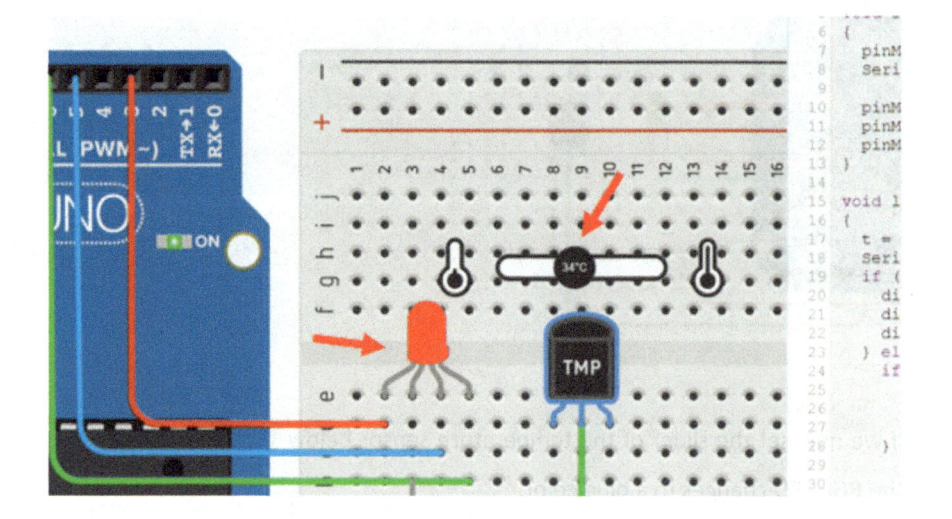

If you are now also rightly curious about the mini-PC Arduino and would like to have more detailed information and more projects about it, I recommend my course "Arduino | Step by Step". You can find more information on the last pages of this book.

Tinkercad | Step by Step

5 Programming with Tinkercad

For the previous electronics project with the Arduino, I gave you the program code that was necessary to tell the Arduino which signal it should send to the LED at which sensor value as already finished text. But surely, you want to learn how to create such a program code. If you don't know the programming language, in this case it's "C++", this can be a bit difficult as a beginner. How good that we have an easier alternative in Tinkercad.

We can program block-based in Tinkercad. This works similarly to how we applied it to the CAD design of the chair in a previous chapter. But there are still differences, of course. In this chapter, we will look at how block-based programming works in Tinkercad and create the program code for the previous Arduino project with the temperature sensor and the RGB LED. This is going to be pretty cool!

To start programming, we simply select the "Code" button in the upper function bar in the Arduino project. A workspace will then open on the right, this is where we will do the programming.

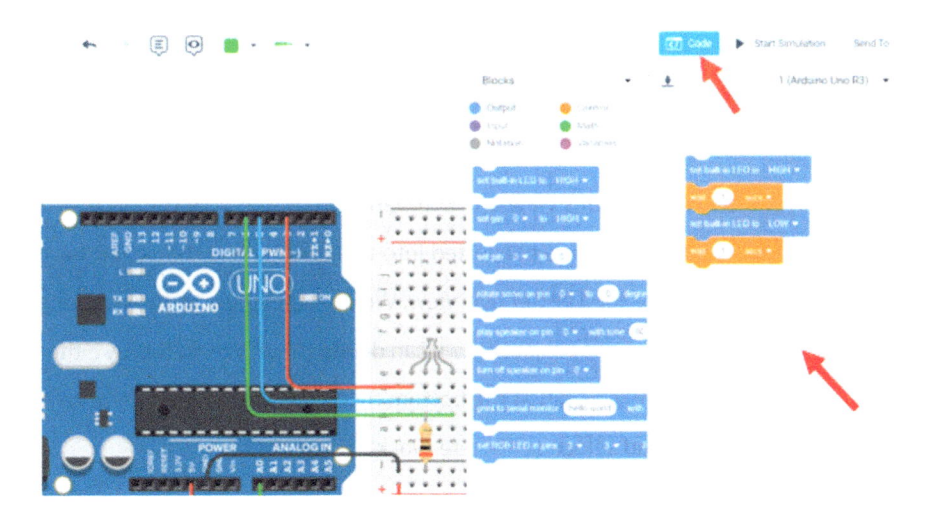

Tinkercad | Step by Step

As we can see, in the upper-left area there are different categories with different colors, which you can click through. In the lower-left area, you will find the default blocks of each category. On the right is our workspace, which already contains two blue and two orange sample blocks.

In the upper area, on the left side, there is another selection menu, which is extremely ingenious because we can switch between text and block. With the option "Blocks + Text" we can display the program code as text to the right of the blocks. This means we don't have to write any program code, but get it automatically generated by the program from our block-based programming. This is extremely helpful for beginners of programming. Great feature!

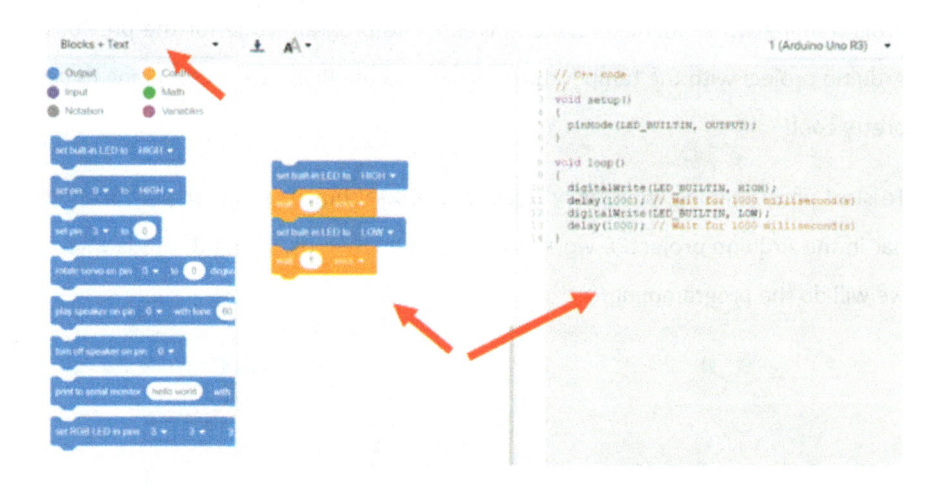

If you like, you can activate this view and compare line by line how the particular statement we create as a block is converted into a program code. However, I will only show the blocks here for a better overview. We don't need the already existing blue and orange blocks for our project, so we can delete them. We do this by either dragging them into the recycle bin at the bottom right, or by clicking on them with the left mouse button and selecting "Delete Block".

Tinkercad | Step by Step

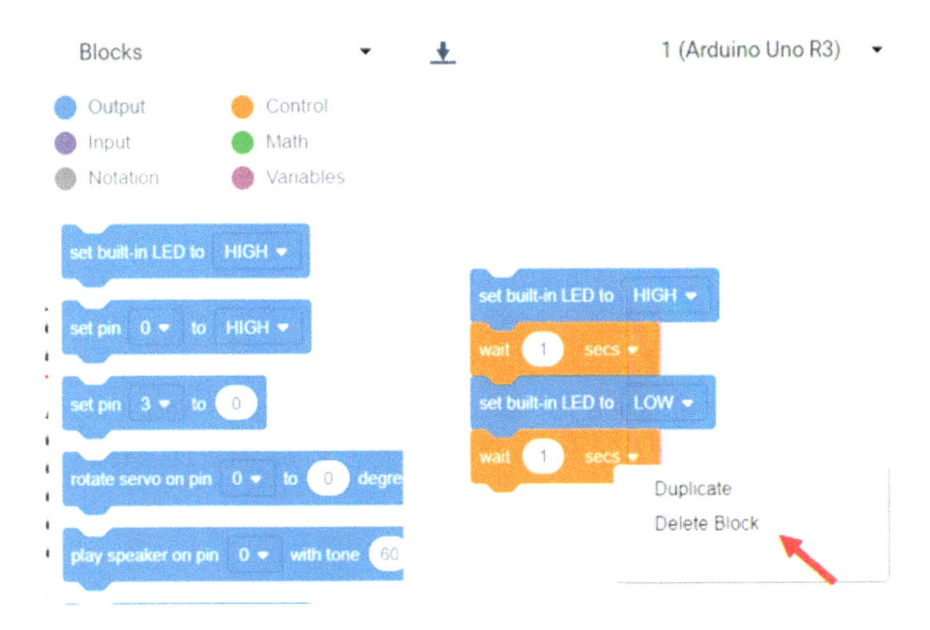

By the way, in the bar in the upper area there is the function "Download Code", with which we can download the program code to transfer it to a real Arduino. On the right side there is another selection menu "Select Device", with which we can set which Arduino we want to program. But this is only relevant if we have created multiple Arduino or other microcontrollers in our project.

Now we start with the programming! As a first step, we want the Arduino to read the value of the temperature sensor. The temperature sensor continuously sends a signal to input A0 of the Arduino (if it is connected here). To make the Arduino read this value, we first create a variable with the letter "t" for temperature. We create this variable in the category "Variables" with the button "Create variable...".

109

Tinkercad | Step by Step

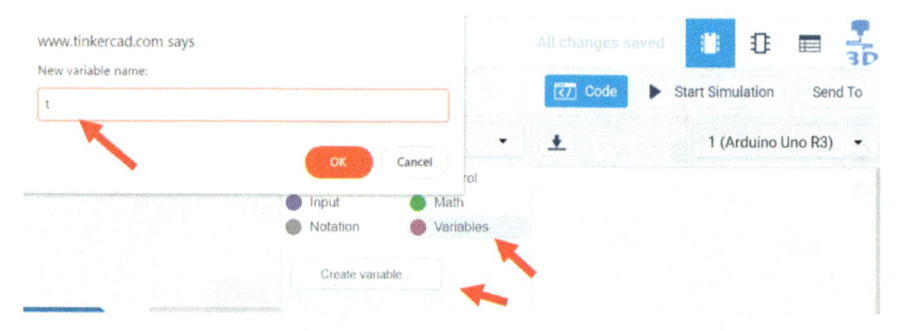

A variable is basically just a placeholder in which we can store a variable, i.e., changeable value. As soon as we have created the variable, the block with the instruction "set t to 0" appears in the same category. We need this block first and therefore drag it into our workspace on the right side.

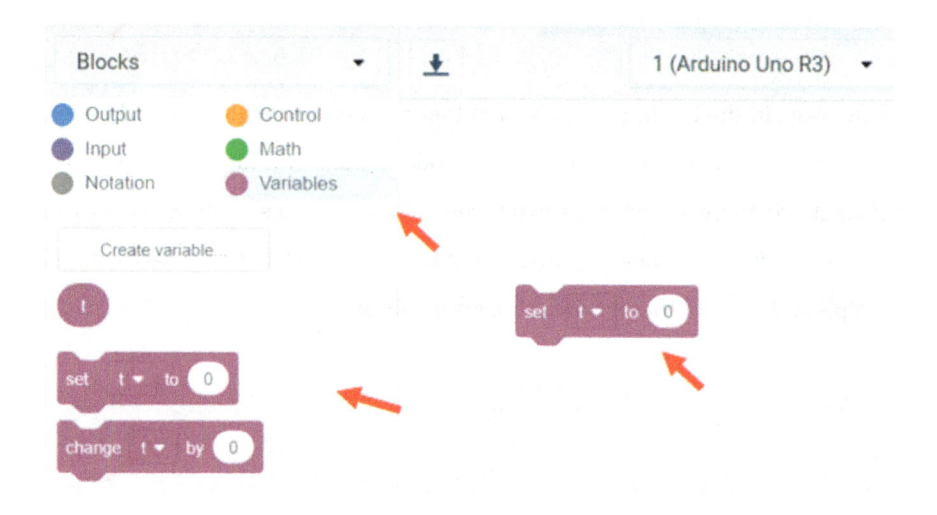

If we would leave the statement as it is, it would mean that we assign the value "0" to the variable "t". But that makes no sense to us. What do we want to assign to the variable instead? Exactly, the temperature that the sensor measures. We get this by commanding the Arduino to read the signal at input A0 – this is where the signal from the temperature sensor arrives in our example. We do this with the command "read analog pin A0" from the category "Input". We can position this command block instead of the 0. Just push it in, it will make a plop sound when that has worked.

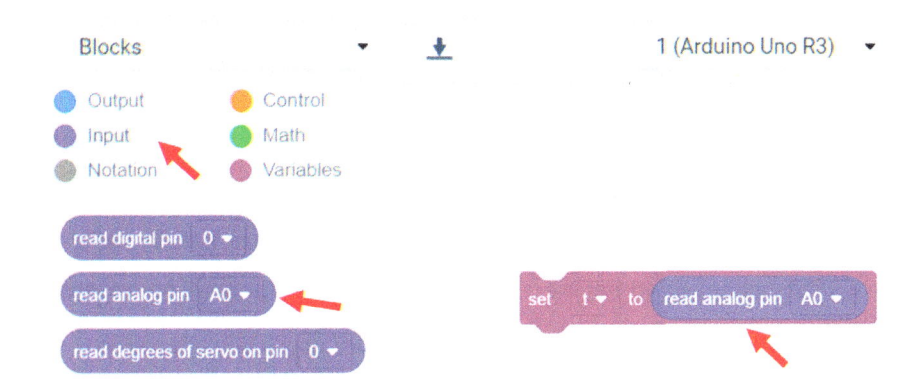

So now the Arduino would assign to the variable "t" the value that the Arduino receives at pin A0 from the temperature sensor. However, the temperature sensor does not send a temperature value in the actual sense, but the sensor only sends a voltage that can be associated with a certain temperature. Which signal the sensor sends, we see in the "serial monitor". For this, we need the command block "print to serial monitor hello world with newline" from the category "Output". We place it below the first block.

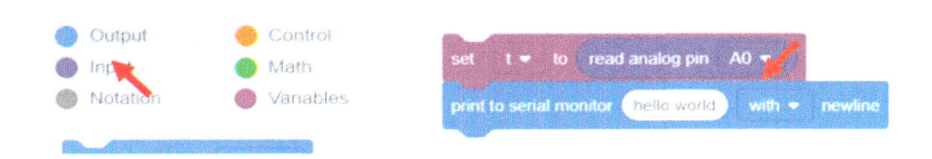

Instead of "hello world" we want to get our sensor value, so we insert a new block with the variable "t" from the category "Variables" and overwrite "hello world".

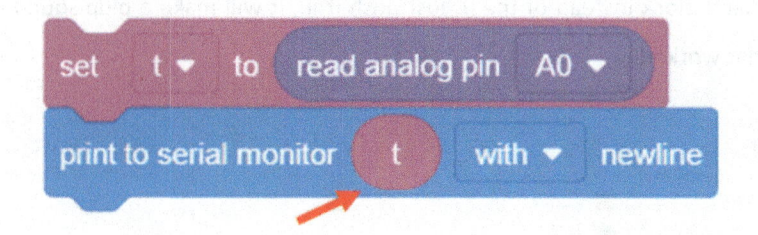

Tinkercad | Step by Step

```
set  t ▼  to  read analog pin  A0 ▼
print to serial monitor   t     with ▼  newline
```

Now we can open the serial monitor in the lower area by clicking on the corresponding button "Serial Monitor" and, as soon as we start the simulation in the upper function bar, we get the respective voltages that the temperature sensor outputs – depending on the temperature.

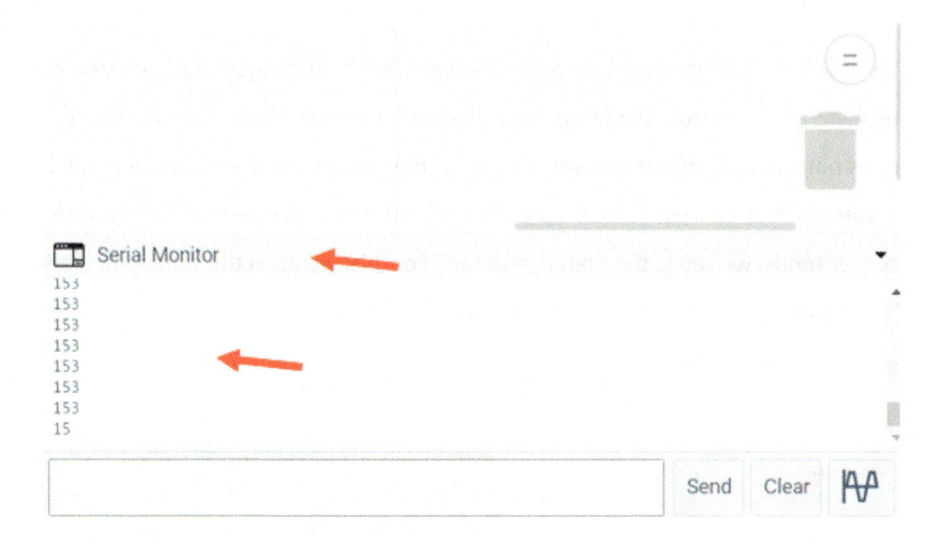

```
Serial Monitor
153
153
153
153
153
153
153
15
                                              Send  Clear
```

Now, while the simulation is running, if we click on the temperature sensor and change its slider, that is, change the temperature, we will see in the serial monitor how the values sent by the temperature sensor to the Arduino change.

Tinkercad | Step by Step

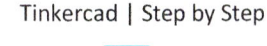

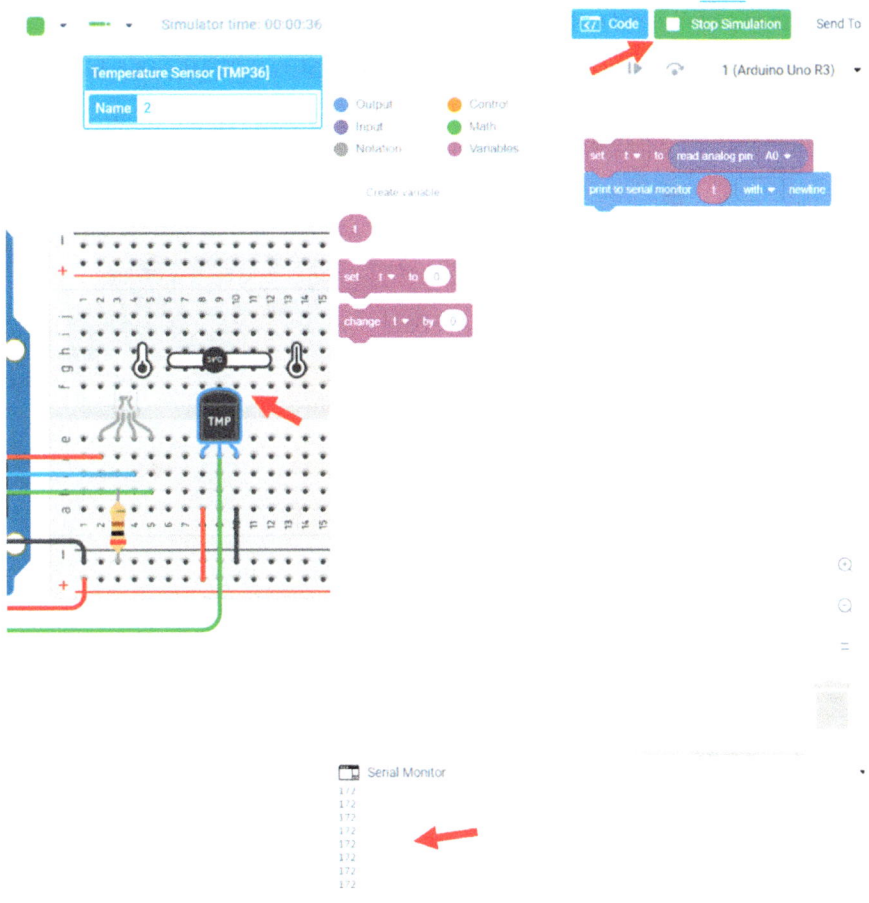

So that we know later which values we need for which temperature, we now set the temperatures 15 °C and 25 °C one after the other and read the value displayed in the serial monitor in each case. We get 135 for 15 °C and 155 for 25 °C.

Now we can end the simulation again and continue with the programming. In the next step, we want to determine that the blue LED lights up if the temperature is below 15 °C, i.e., the value measured by the sensor is below the value 135. For this, we need a statement that is often used in programming. The so-called "if...then" instruction. We even need the "if...then...else" statement here because we want to set other conditions for the other colors of the LED after the first if statement. This statement actually says nothing else than if a certain event – to be defined –

113

Tinkercad | Step by Step

occurs, then a command to be determined is to be executed. If the condition does not occur, something else should follow in case of "else". We add the block "if...then... else" block from the "Control" category to our program code.

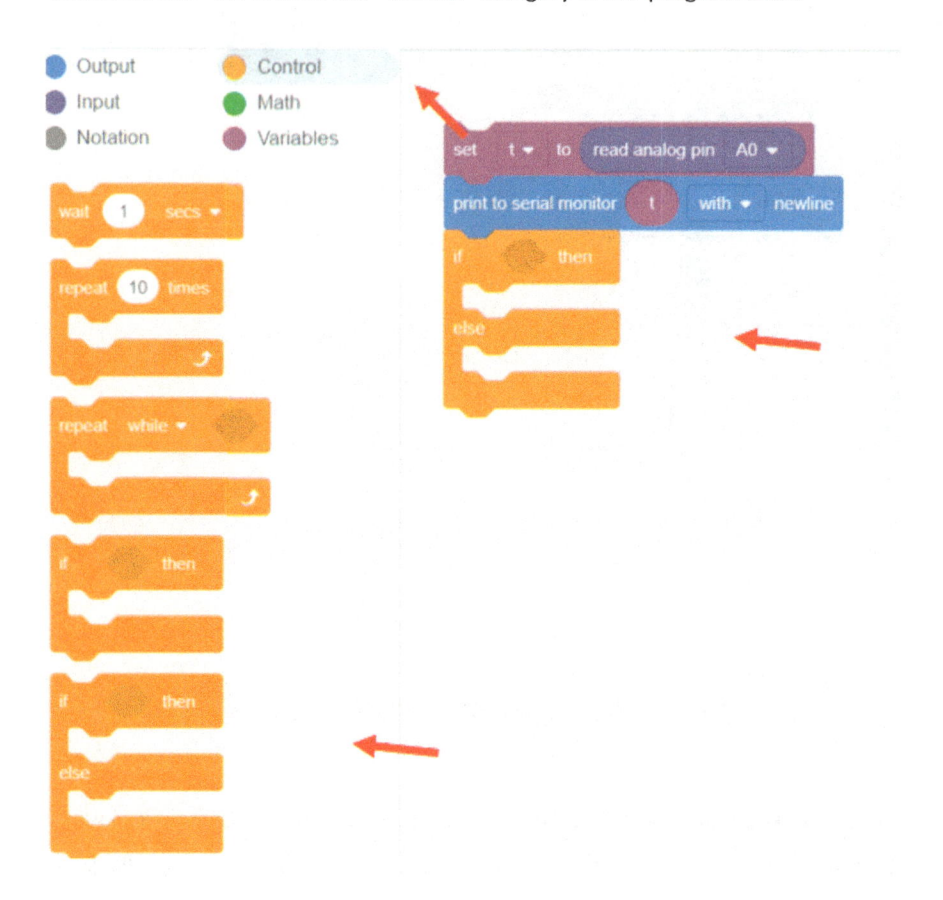

Now we have to determine which condition should be checked and which command should be executed if the condition is met or if the condition is not met. As a condition, we want to check whether the value of the temperature sensor, which we let store in our variable "t" with the first code block, is below 135 or not. That means we have to get a mathematical comparison of two values from the category "Math":

Tinkercad | Step by Step

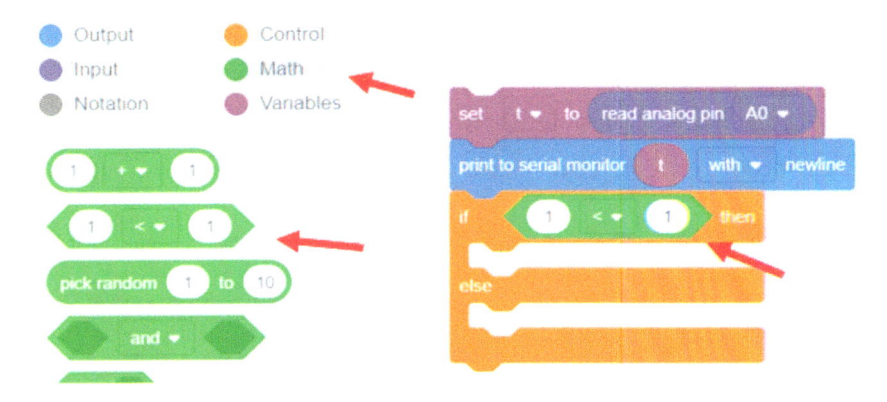

However, we want to avoid comparing two ones, but the variable t and the value 135. We can leave the symbol for "...less than or equal to..." in the middle. Drag the variable "t" into it and simply enter the value 135 with the keyboard.

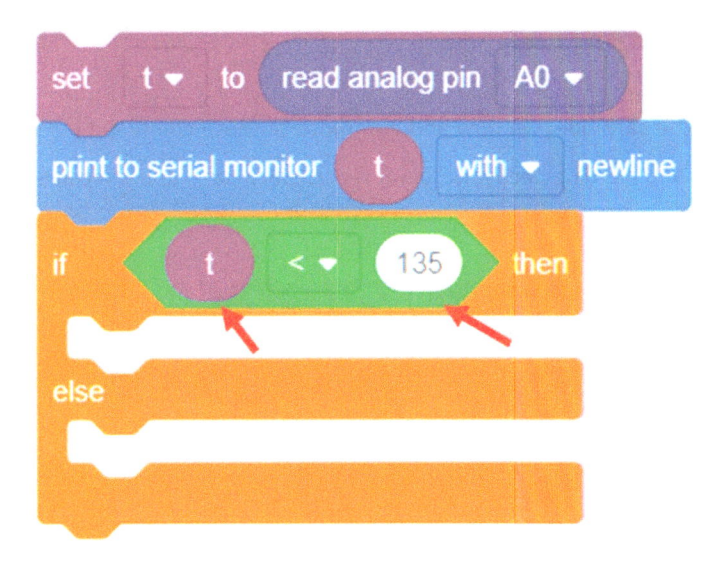

What should happen now if the condition "t < 135" is fulfilled? Exactly, the RGB LED should light up in blue. When does the RGB-LED light up in blue? When the leg labeled "Blue" (the second from the right) receives power from the Arduino. This leg is connected to pin 5 on the Arduino. This again means we need to tell the Arduino in the program code that if the condition is met, it should supply power to

115

pin 5. We do this with the command block "set pin 0 to HIGH" from the "Output" category. Of course, we still have to convert the 0 to a 5. The command "HIGH" on the other hand fits. You can choose between "HIGH" and "LOW". "HIGH" means that a pin receives current, "LOW" means that a pin does not receive current.

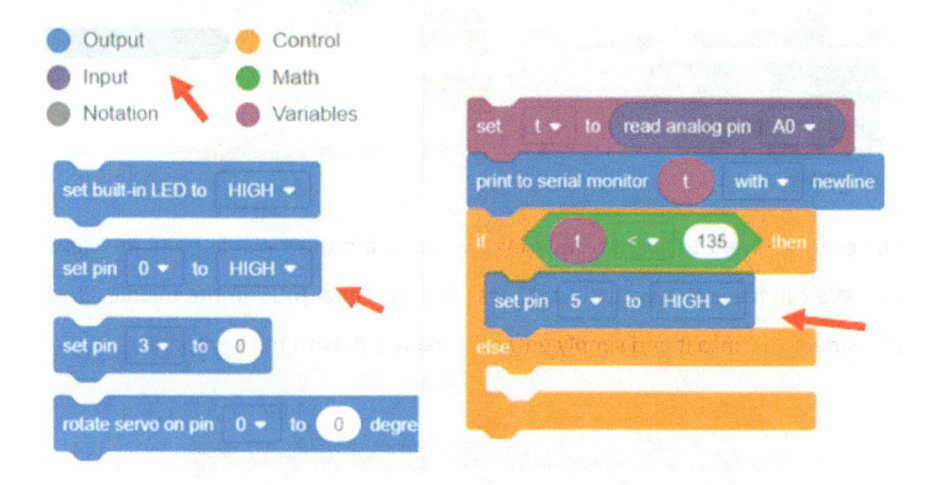

To be on the safe side, we now add two more of these command blocks and set that pin 3 and pin 6 respectively do not receive any current, i.e. receive the signal "LOW".

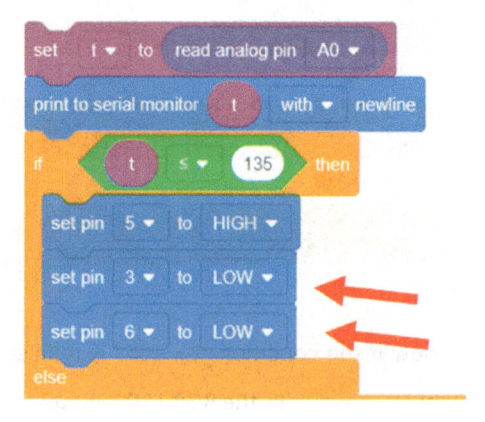

Superb! Now we have created the function that the LED turns blue if the temperature signal falls below the value 135, that is the temperature is below 15 °C.

We now continue with the temperature range between 15 °C and 25 °C, here we want the LED to light up green. The procedure is now relatively identical. We have to create another if-condition, which we insert into the "else" area of the first if-condition. This second if-condition should be checked, if the first condition is not fulfilled. By the way, this is called a nested if-condition. To be more precise, we create another "if...then... else"-condition because we have to consider another case, if this condition is not fulfilled either.

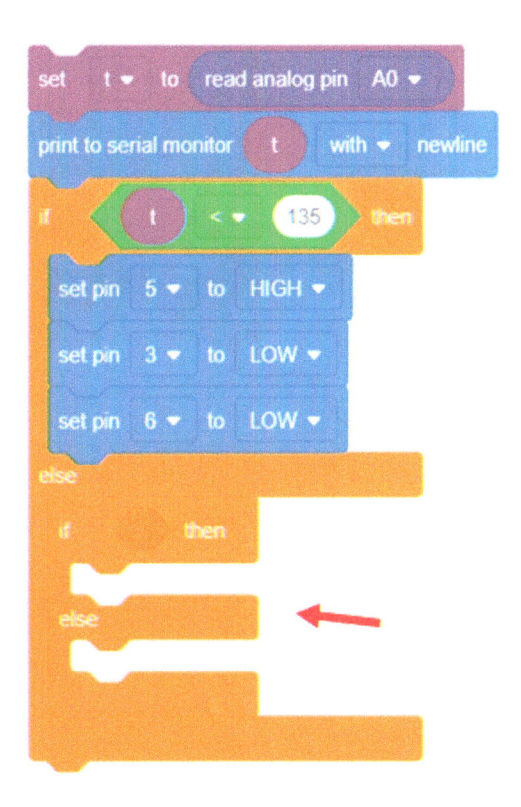

You are now welcome to think on your own about what we need to insert into this block so that we can check the temperature range between 15 °C and 25 °C. The solution will follow shortly.

We need to have two cases checked here, for this we first need a mathematical "and" block.

Tinkercad | Step by Step

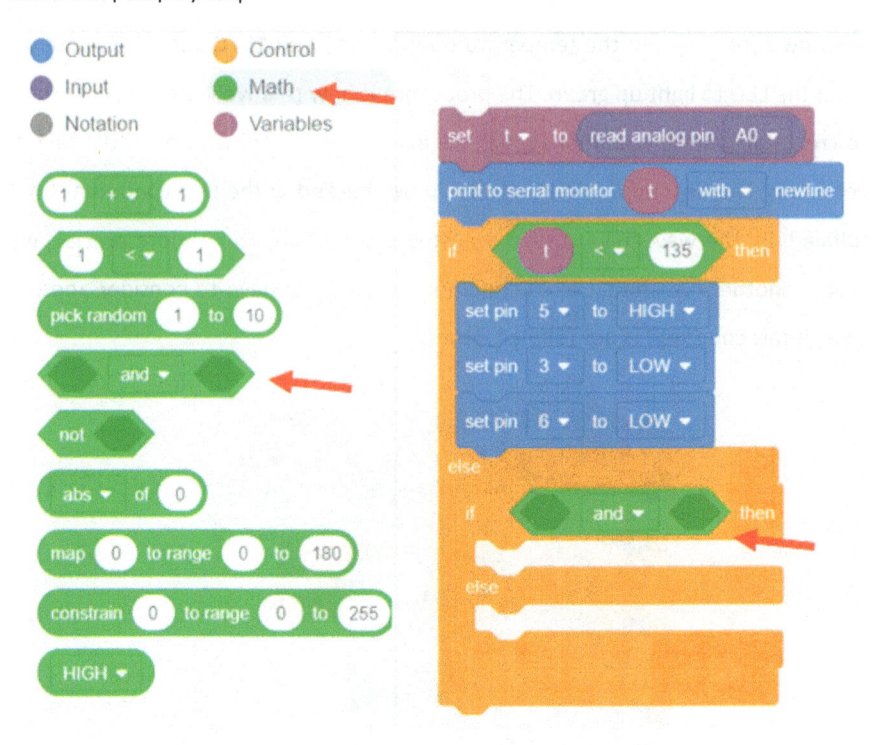

In this, we put the check of the case "t greater than 135" on the left and on the right we put the check of the case "t less than or equal to 155". So, this instruction checks us if the value of the temperature sensor is between the two values 135 and 155.

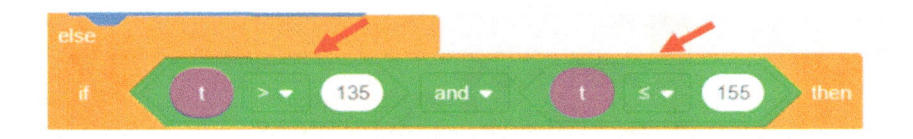

If this condition is met, i.e., the temperature is between 15 °C and 25 °C, the RGB LED should light up green. The leg for the green color is located on the far right and is connected to pin 6 of the Arduino in our circuit. The procedure for the further commands is now identical to the previous one. We have to supply pin 6 with power and de-energize the other two pins.

Tinkercad | Step by Step

Finally, we have to consider the remaining case. Here we have to check if the temperature is above 25 °C, i.e., if the sensor value is above 155. If this is the case, the red LED should light up, i.e., the leg connected to pin 3 should be supplied with power. You can do this on your own. Try it out, that's the best way to learn. The solution will follow soon. Note: We need an if-condition again. But this time only a simple one.

119

Tinkercad | Step by Step

```
set t ▼ to  read analog pin A0 ▼
print to serial monitor  t   with ▼  newline
if  t  ≤ ▼  135  then
    set pin 5 ▼ to HIGH ▼
    set pin 3 ▼ to LOW ▼
    set pin 6 ▼ to LOW ▼
else
    if  t  > ▼  135  and ▼  t  ≤ ▼  155  then
        set pin 5 ▼ to LOW ▼
        set pin 3 ▼ to LOW ▼
        set pin 6 ▼ to HIGH ▼
    else
        if  t  > ▼  155  then
            set pin 5 ▼ to LOW ▼
            set pin 3 ▼ to HIGH ▼
            set pin 6 ▼ to LOW ▼
```

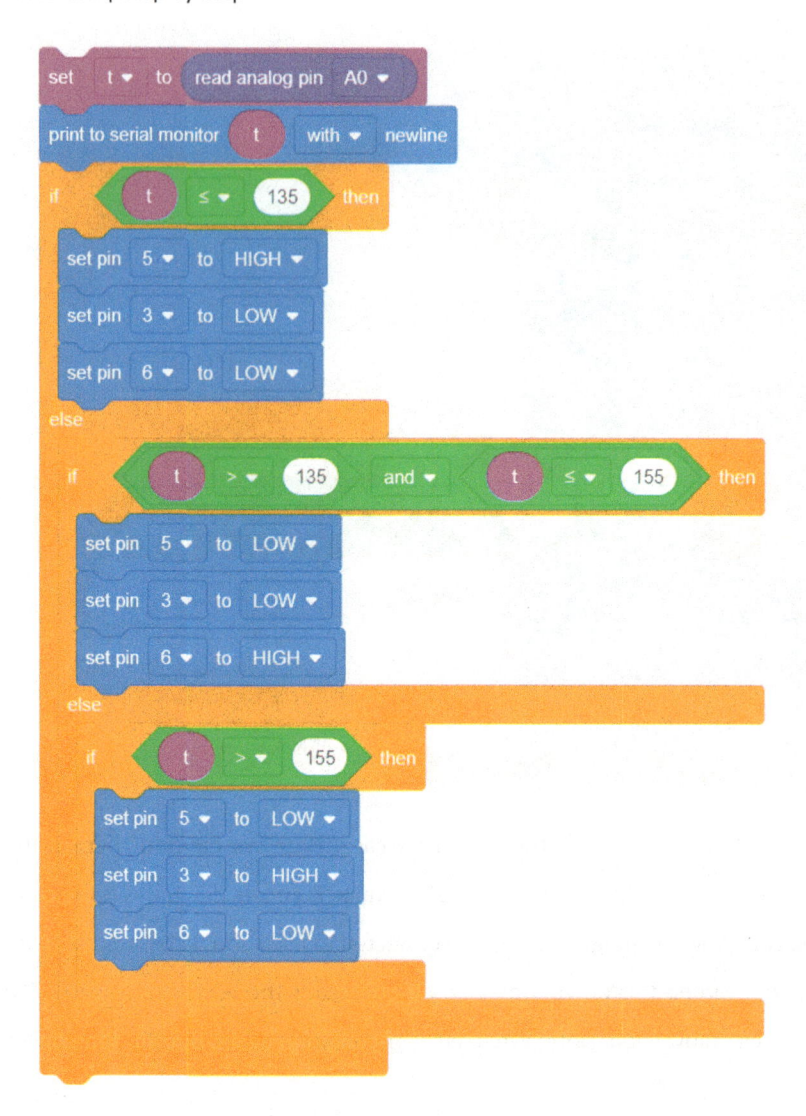

Fantastic! Now we have done it. You can now press "Simulation" and try out with the temperature controller whether the programming was successful. You can also display the program code with "Blocks + Text". That wasn't as hard as you might expected. Flawless! With this chapter, we now finish this beginner course! Congratulations!

Closing words

Excellent! You did it, you worked through the beginner's course for the Tinkercad software. That is a very good achievement!

In this book, I have tried to give you the basic knowledge for working with the software Tinkercad in a simple way and to awaken or strengthen your enthusiasm for CAD design, electronics and programming. I hope that I have succeeded to some extent and that this book has brought you a well understandable and practical introduction to Tinkercad.

The goal of this book was to give you an understanding of what you can create with electronics, programming, and CAD design using Tinkercad on the PC. It should be a book that creates an understanding of the theoretical background knowledge and the practical application.

With this basic course, you should now know everything you need as a beginner to work with Tinkercad! Of course, it makes sense not to stop at this point and look into an advanced book.

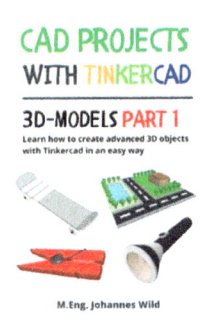

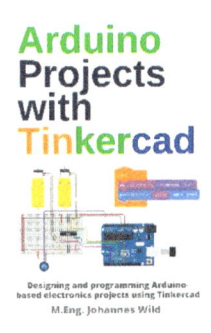

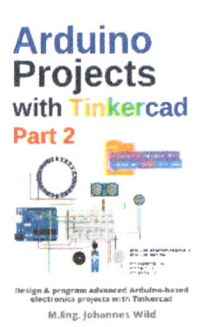

Together, we have accomplished quite a bit in this course! You can be justifiably proud of yourself for getting this far.

If you liked this book, I would be pleased if you leave me a rating and a short feedback, as well as recommend the book! **Thank you very much!**

Books on topics you might also like

All books are available online on the usual sales platforms. It's best to just search for the title, or feel free to visit my author page. Some of the books may not be published yet and will be released or found soon. Take a look at the books of your choice and your copy as e-book or paperback!

3D Printing:

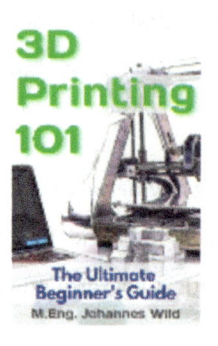

CAD, FEM, CAM (3D Object Creation, Design, Simulation):

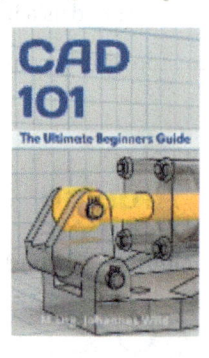

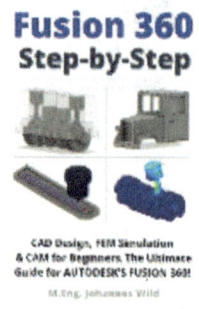

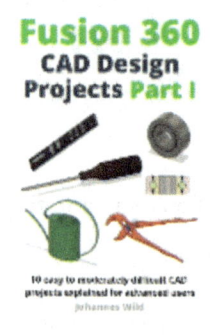

Electrical Engineering:

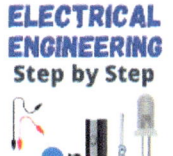

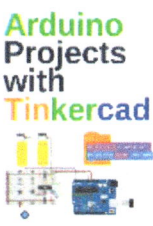

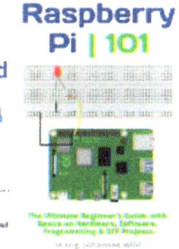

Programming and other Software:

123

Tinkercad | Step by Step

There are also identical video courses for some of these books:

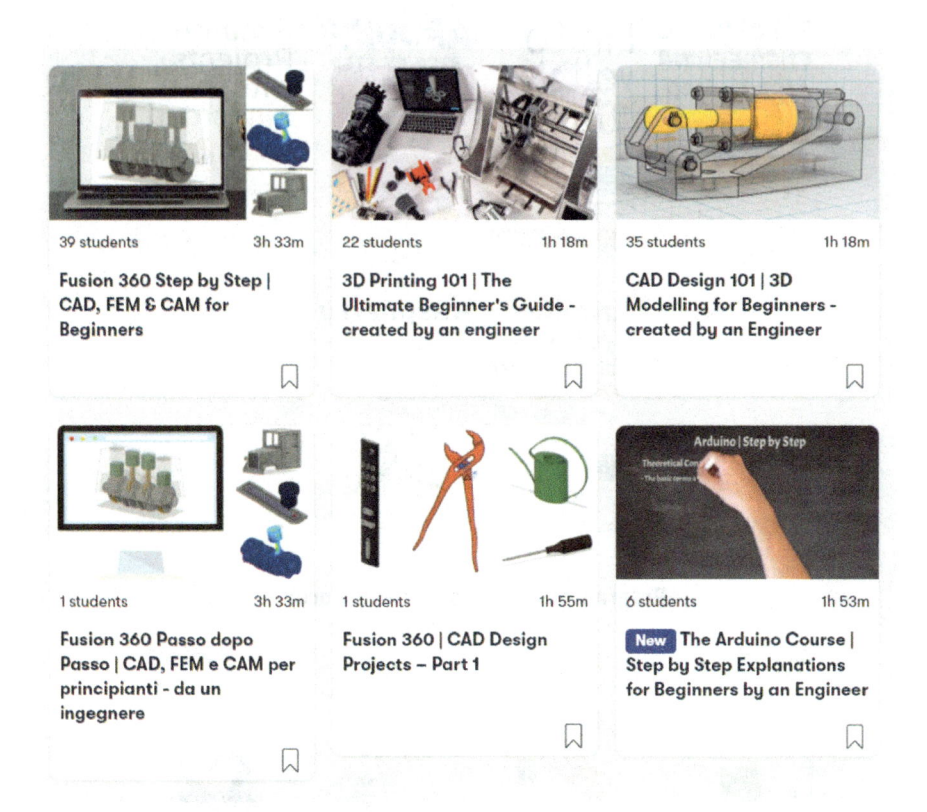

39 students — 3h 33m
Fusion 360 Step by Step | CAD, FEM & CAM for Beginners

22 students — 1h 18m
3D Printing 101 | The Ultimate Beginner's Guide - created by an engineer

35 students — 1h 18m
CAD Design 101 | 3D Modelling for Beginners - created by an Engineer

1 students — 3h 33m
Fusion 360 Passo dopo Passo | CAD, FEM e CAM per principianti - da un ingegnere

1 students — 1h 55m
Fusion 360 | CAD Design Projects – Part 1

6 students — 1h 53m
New The Arduino Course | Step by Step Explanations for Beginners by an Engineer

They are hosted on the learning website: skillshare.com

Be sure to use my following friends & family referral link to get a month of membership for free !

(I will get a little bonus if you choose to stay, so we will be both 😊 Thanks in advance!)

https://www.skillshare.com/r/profile/Johannes-Wild/854541251

It is best to copy the link in your browser to access the free month !

Sign up today and deepen your knowledge!

Imprint of the author / publisher

© 2023

Johannes Wild
c/o RA Matutis
Berliner Straße 57
14467 Potsdam
Germany

Email: 3dtech@gmx.de

This work is protected by copyright

The work, including its parts, is protected by copyright. Any use outside the narrow limits of copyright law without the consent of the author is prohibited. This applies in particular to electronic or other reproduction, translation, distribution and making publicly available. No part of the work may be reproduced, processed or distributed without written permission of the author! All rights reserved.

All information contained in this book has been compiled to the best of our knowledge and has been carefully checked. However, this book is for educational purposes only and does not constitute a recommendation for action. In particular, no warranty or liability is given by the author and publisher for the use or non-use of any information in this book. Trademarks and other rights cited in this book remain the sole property of their respective authors or rights holders.

Thank you so much for choosing this book!

Made in the USA
Monee, IL
19 July 2025